DECODING YOUR TWIN FLAME

Why They Run, Why You Chase, and What the Connection Is Really Awakening in You

Grace Brewster

Copyright

First Edition 2026
ISBN: 978-1-996859-00-1
Self Published

Acknowledgments

This book was not written from theory. It was written from experience: from intensity, confusion, stillness, laughter, restraint, expansion, and the quiet discipline of not collapsing under emotion.

To the journey itself, thank you. You dismantled illusions I didn't know I was holding. You exposed attachment where I thought there was destiny. You demanded growth when I wanted romance. You forced me inward when I would have preferred to decode someone else.

To the catalyst, thank you for activating what was already within me. Whether you knew it or not, you triggered the mirror. You awakened parts of me that had been dormant. You became the contrast that sharpened my awareness. This book would not exist without that spark.

To the readers who are living this dynamic in silence, this is for you. You are not crazy. You are not weak. You are not dramatic. You are navigating something that asks for emotional maturity, energetic discipline, and self-honesty. That is no small thing.

To the version of me who stayed, who detached, who returned to stillness, who refused to shrink, thank you for living it fully enough that I could write it truthfully.

And to the unseen work — the private realizations, the ego dismantling, the quiet growth that no one applauded, you are the real author of these pages.

The question is no longer:
"Is this my twin flame?"

Dedication

For the ones who couldn't leave
and couldn't stay.

For the journey that dismantled you
and rebuilt you stronger.

This is for the becoming.

The question becomes:
"Does this bond allow me to remain myself?"

Table of Contents

Table of Contents

Introduction

Before You Decode

If you picked up this book, chances are you're not looking for entertainment. You're looking for clarity.

Maybe you've felt a connection that doesn't make sense. Maybe it feels spiritual, magnetic, disruptive, or all three at once. Maybe friends have told you to walk away. Maybe online forums told you to wait. Maybe you've been called awakened, obsessed, delusional, chosen, or dramatic — sometimes in the same week.

I'm not here to diagnose you. I'm not here to validate every feeling or dismantle your belief system. I'm here to decode the experience.

I am living the dynamic, observing it, and learning from it. I have not been on this journey for decades. I have not mastered it, but I have watched it carefully enough to see patterns in myself, in others, in the architecture of attachment and awakening.

This book is not about proving whether twin flames are real. It is not about convincing you to stay or leave. It is not about guaranteeing union or predicting separation.

It is about awareness.

Because inside this dynamic, it is very easy to lose perspective. The intensity feels cosmic. The push and pull feel symbolic. The silence feels loaded. The reunion feels fated. The distance feels catastrophic.

And yet, beneath all of it, there is something much more grounded happening.

You are being activated.

This book will peel back the layers. Not to diminish the connection, but to understand it. Not to remove romance, but to separate it from illusion. Not to dismiss the spiritual, but to locate it correctly.

You may recognize yourself as the chaser. You may recognize someone else as the runner. You may question whether this is trauma, destiny, projection, sacred bond, or something else entirely.

We will look at all of it.

Not with panic. Not with fantasy, but with clarity.

Decoding is not about destroying the bond.

It is about understanding what is happening inside you while the bond unfolds.

If you are ready to look honestly, even when it's uncomfortable, then let's begin.

Chapter 1

Before You Call It a Twin Flame

Before you decide what this connection is, you need to notice what it is doing to you.

Most people start with the label. Twin flame. Soulmate. Karmic. Toxic. Destiny. They try to categorize the experience before they've actually observed it. But naming something too quickly can distort it. It turns the experience into a concept, and once it becomes a concept, you stop feeling it clearly.

This book is not here to convince you that you have a twin flame. It is not here to tell you to stay, to leave, to chase, or to detach. It is here for something much simpler and much harder.

It is here to help you observe.

Because before any spiritual explanation enters the picture, something real has already happened. Your emotional baseline shifted. Your nervous system reacted differently than it usually does. You started responding in ways that surprised you. Maybe you felt stronger than ever. Maybe weaker. Maybe calm and destabilized at the same time.

That shift matters more than the label.

A true twin flame dynamic does not begin with fireworks. It begins with recognition, but not the romantic kind. It feels like something in you woke up and started paying attention. Not just to them, but to yourself.

You may notice that you are not behaving the way you normally behave in relationships. You might feel drawn without effort. Or you might feel activated, irritated, or unsettled. You might feel both expansion and contraction happening at once. It doesn't follow ordinary dating logic.

That's where decoding begins.

Not by asking, "Are they my twin flame?"

But by asking, "What is this connection revealing about me?"

Because whatever this is — twin flame, soul connection, projection, unfinished emotional pattern, it is interacting with your internal architecture. And that interaction is the real story.

Throughout this book, we will not rush to conclusions. We will move layer by layer. Emotional shifts. Behavioral patterns. Push and pull.

Intensity. Silence. Stillness. Obsession. Detachment. All of it.

This book is a mirror.

Not only to explain your connection, but to let you see it in a way you haven't before.

If something in your life has felt intense, confusing, or undeniable, this is where the decoding quietly begins.

You don't need to decide anything yet. You only need to watch.

If this connection feels different, if it feels like it's rearranging you from the inside out, then you're in the right place.

Let's decode it slowly.

Chapter 2

When Your Emotional Baseline Changes

Most connections enter your life and stay on the surface. You enjoy them. You evaluate them. You decide whether they fit. They rise and fall within your normal emotional range.

But sometimes, one connection does something different. It doesn't just create feelings: It alters your baseline.

At least, that's what I experienced.

I didn't just feel attraction. I felt rearranged.

I woke up, and something inside me had shifted. The world looked the same, but my internal atmosphere had changed. Silence felt heavier. My body carried a current I couldn't explain. Even when nothing was happening, something was happening.

I wasn't simply interested. I was altered.

Before that connection, I knew my rhythm. I knew how I reacted to affection, to distance, to rejection. I knew how long it took me to detach. I knew what bored me and what excited me. I thought I understood my own emotional architecture.

Then my reactions stopped following my old script.

There were moments when I felt calm in situations that would normally trigger anxiety. Other times, I felt destabilized in places that should have felt safe. I could feel expansion and heaviness at the same time. It didn't make logical sense.

It wasn't just love.

It was activation.

When your emotional baseline shifts, your nervous system is responding to something it recognizes as significant. Not necessarily safe. Not necessarily forever. Just significant.

And significance feels different from chemistry.

Chemistry is loud. It burns fast. It demands attention.

A baseline shift is quieter. It seeps in. You may not notice it immediately. But over time, you realize you are no longer the same version of yourself you were before the connection.

For me, it changed my tolerance. I could no longer pretend with shallow interactions. I became more aware of my own patterns. More aware of my attachments. More aware of the way I chased intensity.

It wasn't dramatic on the outside.

But internally, something had recalibrated.

This is where many people misinterpret what is happening.

They assume intensity means compatibility. They assume disruption means destiny. They assume confusion means karmic debt.

But the emotional baseline shift is not a conclusion. It is a mirror.

The real question isn't, "Are they my twin flame?"

It's, "Why did my internal system respond this strongly?"

If a connection is deeply significant, whatever label you give it, it won't just create longing. It will change your calibration. Your tolerance for superficial connections decreases. Your awareness increases. You may even lose interest in things that once stimulated you.

You are not becoming dramatic.

You are becoming precise.

The shift may feel intoxicating. It may feel destabilizing. It may feel expansive. It may feel like floating. It may feel like heaviness in the chest that you cannot explain.

All of that is information.

Before deciding what this connection is, observe what it has done to you. Because decoding does not begin with the other person.

It begins when you stop being your old emotional self.

And that moment, not the label, is where the real story starts.

Chapter 3

What Is Actually Pulling You?

There is a moment in every intense connection when your attention quietly shifts outward. You stop living your own rhythm and begin studying theirs. You notice how long it takes them to respond. You replay the way they looked at you. You measure the warmth in their voice. You analyze the silence.

It feels natural. Of course you would try to understand the person who just disrupted your emotional landscape.

But this is where most people begin decoding the wrong thing.

Because the pull you feel is not only about them.

It is about what was activated inside you.

There is a difference between attraction and activation. Attraction feels enjoyable. It moves toward pleasure. Activation is different. Activation wakes something up. It heightens perception. It rearranges your nervous system. It exposes dormant parts of you that were quietly asleep.

Activation can feel like destiny. It can feel like fate. It can feel like recognition. And because it feels powerful, we immediately assume the power belongs to the other person.

But often, the intensity is your own system responding to expansion.

Psychologically, intense bonds stimulate attachment pathways. They awaken memory, longing, fear, desire, imagination. They stimulate the part of you that wants to secure, to understand, to define. The brain does not like uncertainty, especially when emotion is involved. So it tries to create a narrative quickly: This must be my twin flame. This must be the one. This must mean something.

Energetically, intensity feels even bigger. It feels like frequency alignment. Like electricity in the chest. Like magnetism. Like being seen beyond the surface. When that happens, the body interprets it as significance.

And sometimes it is significant.

But significance does not automatically mean permanence. Intensity does not automatically mean compatibility. Activation does not automatically mean union.

This is where decoding begins.

Instead of asking, "Why are they acting this way?" the deeper question becomes, "What is this connection awakening in me?"

Are you feeling expanded or destabilized? Are you feeling more yourself or less grounded? Are you calm beneath the intensity, or anxious beneath the excitement?

These distinctions matter.

Because when a connection is aligned, your system may feel stimulated, but it does not feel fragmented. You may feel excitement, but not erosion. You may feel depth, but not loss of self.

When a connection is misaligned, the intensity often overrides clarity. You begin tolerating confusion because the spark feels worth it. You excuse inconsistency because the chemistry feels rare. You convince yourself that volatility equals depth.

Many people mistake nervous system arousal for spiritual recognition. But arousal and recognition are not the same.

Recognition feels steady underneath the charge. Arousal feels urgent and unstable.

If you slow down and sit quietly, what remains when the texting stops? What remains when the person is not physically present? Does the connection feel grounded inside you, or does it feel like it disappears unless they reappear?

These questions are not meant to invalidate your experience. They are meant to return power to you.

Because decoding your twin flame does not begin with analyzing their behavior.

It begins with observing your own.

When you notice that your mood depends entirely on their responses, something is being revealed. When you notice that your body relaxes in their presence rather than tightens, something is being revealed. When you notice that you are becoming more self-aware instead of more self-abandoning, something is being revealed.

You do not need to label it yet.

You only need to notice.

The pull is information. The intensity is information. Your reaction to both is information. And once you understand what is being activated inside you, the connection becomes clearer — not smaller, not less magical, but clearer.

That clarity is where real decoding begins.

The truth is, intensity does not automatically equal compatibility.

Sometimes it equals activation.

There are connections that feel magnetic not because the other person is "the one," but because they awaken something that was dormant. A hunger. A memory. A version of you that had been quiet for years.

Psychologically, this can look like attachment. Your nervous system gets stimulated. Dopamine rises. Anticipation becomes addictive. The brain starts scanning for signs. You replay conversations. You anticipate messages. You feel highs and lows that seem disproportionate to what is actually happening.

Energetically, it feels even bigger. It feels like fate. Like destiny. Like something ancient just came online. Your body reacts before your logic can catch up.

And this is where many people get lost.

Because when something activates you deeply, the mind wants to explain it quickly. It wants a label. Twin flame. Soulmate. Karma. Trauma bond. Destiny.

But activation is not a label. It is a signal.

The signal is not saying, "Chase them."

The signal is saying, "Something inside you is waking up."

That is a very different message.

And this is where many people get lost.

When I began to sit with the sensation instead of the storyline, I noticed something surprising. The intensity did not disappear. It shifted. It stopped feeling like desperation and started feeling like expansion.

It wasn't about possessing the person.

It was about meeting the part of me that came alive in their presence.

And that changes the decoding entirely.

Because once you understand that some connections are mirrors for your own expansion, you stop trying to control them. You start observing them.

And observation brings clarity.

What makes this dynamic confusing is that both layers are happening at the same time.

On the psychological level, your attachment system is activated. If you lean anxious, you feel pulled forward. If you lean avoidant, you feel the urge to retreat. If you are secure, you might simply observe the shift and feel curious.

But the body reacts before philosophy does.

You check your phone more often. You read tone into short replies. You feel expanded when they lean in and contracted when they pull back. This is biology. It is not madness.

At the same time, something subtler is moving underneath.

Energetically, you may feel recognition before you have evidence. You may feel familiarity without history. You may sense that this person touches something ancient in you, even if you have only known them for weeks.

This is where people rush to mystical conclusions.

But the energetic layer is not there to override the psychological one. It is there to illuminate it.

A twin flame dynamic, whether soul-based or monadic, does not cancel your nervous system. It magnifies it.

And that is the part no one prepares you for.

If the connection activates your abandonment wound, it will feel cosmic.

If it activates your need for validation, it will feel destined.

If it activates your deepest expansion, it will feel like awakening.

The experience is real.

But the interpretation requires decoding.

I learned that the hard way.

There were moments when I thought intensity meant permanence. When I believed that because something felt larger than life, it had to last forever. But intensity is a spark. Permanence is architecture. They are not the same.

And this is where balance matters.

Psychologically, you must ask:
What part of me is being activated?

Energetically, you must ask:
Is this expanding me or consuming me?

Those two questions alone can shift everything.

Because decoding is not about proving that someone is your twin flame.

It is about understanding what the connection is doing to your inner structure.

When you begin to see that clearly, you stop chasing labels. You start reading patterns.

And patterns never lie.

Chapter 4

Why It Feels Different From Everything Else

There is a reason this connection does not feel like a normal attraction. It does not sit in the same category as a crush, a relationship, or even love as you have known it before. Something about it bypasses logic. It arrives fully formed. It feels familiar before it feels safe.

At least that is how it happened for me.

What surprised me most was not the intensity. I've always been capable of deep feeling. What surprised me was how quickly it rearranged my internal world. It was as if a frequency I had never heard before suddenly turned on , and once I heard it, I could not unhear it. It didn't ask for permission. It didn't build slowly. It simply existed.

When something like this enters your life, it doesn't just touch your emotions. It touches your identity. You begin to question who you were before it. You notice your reactions more closely. You observe your own behavior as if you are watching yourself from a slight distance. Even silence with this person can feel charged, not dramatic, but heightened. A kind of awareness that sharpens everything.

Psychologically, intense connections can activate attachment patterns, old wounds, unmet needs, and long-buried narratives about love. If you feel anxious, it may awaken longing. If you lean avoidant, it may awaken retreat. If you are independent and grounded, it may still disturb the equilibrium you thought was stable.

Energetically, however, it can feel like recognition. The body reacts before the mind can explain it. The nervous system becomes alert. Time feels distorted. Presence feels amplified. You may feel calm and electrified at the same time. You may feel pulled without understanding why.

This is where most people get confused.

They mistake activation for destiny. Or they dismiss recognition as fantasy. Both reactions are incomplete.

Intensity alone does not make something sacred. Familiarity alone does not make something fate. And disruption alone does not make something toxic. The human system is complex. It can create powerful sensations for many reasons.

So before you decide what this connection means, pause.

Instead of asking, "Are they my twin flame?" Ask, "What part of me is being awakened right now?"

Is it your desire to be seen? Your fear of abandonment? Your longing for expansion? Your resistance to intimacy? Your hunger for something beyond the ordinary?

At least in my experience, the connection did not give me answers. It revealed questions I didn't know I carried.

This is where decoding truly begins.

Not by labeling the other person. Not by romanticizing the experience. But by observing the shift inside you. Because what feels like "them" may be something much closer.

And until you understand that, the intensity will always feel larger than your own authority.

Chapter 5

Projection or Recognition?

There comes a moment in this kind of connection when you begin to wonder: Am I seeing them… or am I seeing something inside myself?

At first, everything feels clear. You feel drawn. You feel alive. You feel expanded. Their presence lights something up in you that hasn't been touched in a long time, maybe ever. And because it feels so rare, you assume it must be about them.

I did.

I thought the intensity meant they carried something extraordinary. I thought the pull meant destiny. I thought the calm and the electricity meant we were made from the same star.

But as time went on, a subtle shift occurred. Slowly, very slowly, I began to notice something.

The qualities I admired most in them were qualities I was already becoming. The freedom I felt around them was a freedom I was learning to claim. The confidence I thought they triggered in me was already waking up inside me.

That's when the question shifted: was I truly seeing them, or was I really seeing myself?

Projection isn't a bad word. It doesn't mean you're delusional. It doesn't mean the connection isn't real. It simply means that sometimes we place our own unfinished expansion onto another person. We see in them what we are ready to awaken in ourselves.

Recognition, on the other hand, feels different.

Recognition doesn't inflate the other person. It doesn't make them a savior or a missing piece. It doesn't feel like you will collapse without them. It feels steady. It feels mutual. It feels like two people standing whole, not leaning.

The confusion happens because projection can feel magical. Recognition feels calm.

Projection feels intoxicating. Recognition feels grounded. Projection needs movement — texts, signs, synchronicities, reassurance. Recognition can sit in silence and not panic.

I had to ask myself: when I felt the pull, was I expanding... or was I reaching?

There is no shame in either answer, but the answer changes everything.
If you are projecting, the work is inward. If you recognize the connection, you can breathe.

And sometimes this is the part no one talks about. It begins as a projection and matures into recognition.

That is part of decoding.

You are not trying to prove the connection. You are trying to understand what is activating in you.

Because the moment you stop needing them to validate what you feel, something shifts. The energy softens. The urgency dissolves. What remains is either clarity... or silence.

Both are answers.

There were nights when I would lie in bed replaying a single moment, the way she laughed, the way she pulled her hand away after five minutes, the way silence between us didn't feel empty. I would ask myself, Was that connection… or was that hope?

No one sees this part. The part where you sit with your own thoughts and don't know whether you are remembering something real or remembering how you felt.

That distinction matters.

Because sometimes what we miss isn't the person. It's who we were when we were with them.

I noticed that when I was around her, I felt sharper. More aware. More awake. Not because she was doing anything extraordinary — sometimes she was quiet, sometimes distant, but because something inside me was lit up.

That's when I had to be honest.

Was I attached to her… or to the version of myself that appeared in her presence?

That question is uncomfortable. It doesn't accuse anyone. It doesn't blame the other person. It simply turns the mirror slightly.

And in that mirror, I saw something unexpected. I wasn't incomplete. I wasn't abandoned. I wasn't chasing.

I was expanding.

Projection is like holding on to something. Recognition is like discovering something.

When it's a projection, you fear losing them. When it's recognition, you trust what is unfolding, even if it walks away.

That's the intimacy of decoding. It's not about labeling the connection. It's about watching yourself inside it.

When It Doesn't Feel Like "Just a Crush"

There are connections that excite you. There are connections that flatter you. There are connections that make you feel chosen. But then there is this one.

The one that doesn't just make your heart race: it rearranges something inside you.

It's not only an attraction. It's recognition. And recognition can be quiet.

I remember realizing that this wasn't about wanting someone to want me back. I had experienced that before. I knew what it felt like to be chased. I knew what it felt like to chase. That dance was familiar.

But this connection was different.

It wasn't about possession. It wasn't about validation. It wasn't even about romance in the traditional sense.

It was the feeling of being internally shifted.

You go home after seeing them, and something feels altered. You don't always know what. You just know you're not exactly the same as you were that morning.

That's when confusion begins because if it were only chemistry, you could categorize it. If it were only an attachment, you could work on it. If it were only fantasy, it would eventually fade.

But this lingers.

And here's the part no one talks about:

Sometimes the intensity isn't about the other person at all. Sometimes it's about the parts of you that are waking up because of them. That's why the experience feels sacred and destabilizing at the same time.

You don't just want them. You want to understand what just happened to you.

Chapter 6

Why This Connection Feels Different

At some point in this dynamic, the question shifts. It's no longer, "Is this real?" Instead, it becomes, "Why does this feel so different from anything I've experienced before?" That question is quieter, but much deeper.

Most people who find themselves in a twin flame connection have loved before. They have felt attraction, heartbreak, chemistry, and even obsession. They know what romance feels like. They know what attachment feels like. Yet this one does not sit in the same category. It feels layered, almost as if the present moment is carrying something older inside it. The conversation is happening now, but the emotional weight feels ancient.

What makes it confusing is that the intensity is not always tied to what is actually happening between the two of you. Sometimes, very little is happening externally. There might not even be a relationship. There might not be daily communication. And yet internally, something is moving.

That is what makes people question themselves.

Because if nothing concrete is happening, why does it feel so significant? Psychologically, we can say that certain attachment patterns are being activated. Energetically, we can describe it as recognition. Emotionally, it feels like remembering something you cannot logically prove. But those explanations, while helpful, do not fully capture the lived experience.

The lived experience feels like being seen in a way that is both comforting and destabilizing. It feels like standing in front of someone

25

who reflects parts of you that you didn't even realize were visible. There can be magnetism, but also discomfort. There can be warmth, but also the urge to pull back. It is rarely simple.

At least that's how it unfolded for me.

What surprised me most was not the intensity of the connection itself, but what it awakened inside me. It stirred ambition, creativity, and courage. It also exposed insecurity, longing, and fear. It was not just about wanting the other person. It was about witnessing parts of myself that had been dormant until this dynamic activated them.

That is why this kind of connection feels rare. Not because it is always romantic or perfect, but because it moves something inside you that does not move easily.

When something shifts at that depth, you cannot pretend it didn't happen. Even if the other person steps back. Even if circumstances change. Even if the dynamic moves in and out of form.

The feeling remains as evidence that something in you was touched.

And that is where decoding truly begins, not with proving the connection, but with understanding what it awakened within you.

Chapter 7

Why the Connection Feels Bigger Than the Person

There is a moment in most twin flame dynamics when you pause and quietly ask yourself, Why does this feel so big?

Sometimes the conversations are ordinary. The time spent together may not even be dramatic. You may not talk every day. You may not even be physically close. And yet, the feeling inside you feels disproportionate to the reality of what is happening.

That contrast can be confusing.

You look at the facts, and they seem small. You look at your internal experience, and it feels enormous. This is where many people start questioning themselves.

You might think, Am I exaggerating this? Am I creating something that isn't there? And because the outer story often looks simple, the inner intensity can make you feel irrational.

But intensity does not automatically mean fantasy.

Sometimes it means something inside you has been activated.

When a connection feels bigger than the person, it often isn't about the other person's personality. It is about what the connection touches inside you. It can awaken longing, identity, old wounds, dormant desire, creativity, purpose, or even parts of yourself that you had kept hidden.

The person becomes the spark, but the fire is yours.

That distinction is important.

If you confuse the spark for the source, you will chase the person. If you recognize the fire as yours, you begin to decode the experience instead of being consumed by it.

And this is where the dynamic becomes powerful instead of destabilizing.

The intensity can also feel addictive.

Not because you are weak. Not because you are delusional. But because the nervous system does not always know the difference between deep emotional activation and chemical attachment.

When a twin flame dynamic begins, it often disrupts your baseline. You may sleep differently. Eat differently. Think differently. Music sounds amplified. Colors feel brighter. Your body feels alert, alive, charged. Even silence with that person can feel electric.

That state is powerful.

And the body likes powerful.

What many people call "fate" can sometimes also be adrenaline. What feels like destiny can also be dopamine. The mind starts replaying moments, analyzing tone, re-reading messages, and remembering tiny gestures. The smallest interaction carries weight because your system has been sensitized.

It does not mean the connection is fake. It means your body has registered it as significant. And once significance is registered, the system wants more.

This is where decoding becomes necessary.

If you do not understand what is happening inside you, you can mistake intensity for compatibility. You can mistake longing for alignment. You can mistake emotional highs and lows for depth.

Sometimes the pull is not about the other person at all. Sometimes it is about how that person disrupted your emotional equilibrium.

There is a difference between feeling expanded and feeling hooked.

Expansion feels steady underneath the intensity. Hooking feels anxious underneath the intensity.

Both can look identical from the outside.

That is why people around you may not understand. They see the circumstances. You feel the charge.

And the charge is real.

But real does not always mean permanent.

When you begin to observe your own reactions instead of only focusing on the other person's behavior, something shifts. The experience becomes less about "Why are they doing this?" and more about "What is happening inside me right now?"

That question changes everything.

Because twin flame dynamics are not only about union. They are also about regulation. And if the connection destabilizes you more than it strengthens you, that is information, not failure, not tragedy, just information.

The addiction fades when awareness grows.

And awareness does not kill the connection. It clarifies it.

Neurologically, your brain reacts as if something profoundly meaningful is happening. The reward system lights up — dopamine, oxytocin, sometimes even adrenaline. But it's not just attraction. It feels like recognition. Your nervous system says, "I know this." Even if you can't logically explain why. That familiarity can create calm... or intensity... depending on what it touches inside you.

Emotionally, mirroring exposes both beauty and wound. When someone reflects your joy, your humor, your depth, you feel expanded. When they reflect your insecurity, your fear of abandonment, your need for reassurance, you feel exposed. That's why twin-flame-like dynamics feel both magical and destabilizing. You're not just being loved. You're being seen.

Energetically, what people describe as "magnetic pull" is often a form of resonance. When two nervous systems sync with similar rhythms, emotional ranges, and depths, it creates a loop. It feels like merging. Time shifts. Silence feels full instead of empty. Sometimes you even describe it as floating or dissolving.

But here's the deeper layer:

When someone mirrors you that deeply, they activate parts of you that were dormant. Not because they gave you something, but because they reflected something back.

And that's why it feels so powerful.

It's not just romance. It's recognition of self through another body.

That's what makes it intense. That's what makes it sacred. And that's what makes it confusing.

Because when the mirror steps away, you're left asking:

Was it them?

Or was it me seeing myself clearly for the first time?

That's where decoding begins.

The "runner and chaser" dynamic does not begin the way people think it does.

It does not begin with someone cold and someone desperate.

It begins with impact.

Two people meet, and something opens. For one, the opening feels exhilarating. For the other, the opening feels destabilizing. Both feel it. They just interpret it differently.

The one who feels expanded may lean closer. They want to explore it. Understand it. Deepen it. The intensity feels like truth.

The one who feels destabilized may lean back. Not because they do not care, but because something inside them has been activated faster than they are ready for.

One moves toward. One moves away. But here is what most people miss: the roles are not fixed personalities. They are nervous system responses.

When connection moves too quickly for someone's emotional capacity, distance becomes a form of regulation. When distance appears, the other nervous system reacts to the absence. And what was once expansion becomes pursuit.

The chaser is often not chasing a person. They are chasing the feeling of wholeness that appeared when the connection felt mutual.

The runner is often not running from love. They are running from overwhelm.

The more one pursues, the more the other feels pressure. The more one withdraws, the more the other feels abandoned. A loop forms. And the loop can last years if no one steps outside of it.

What makes it confusing is that both people may still feel the bond.

They may laugh effortlessly when together. They may feel peace in silence. They may sense something undeniable. Yet when intimacy deepens, one system accelerates and the other retreats.

It is not about who loves more.

It is about who can tolerate closeness without losing themselves.

And sometimes, the chaser believes they are the stronger one because they are willing to feel everything. But often the chase is fueled by fear of losing the experience. Meanwhile, the runner may appear detached, but internally they may feel just as much, only without the tools to stay steady inside it.

This is where decoding becomes mature.

Instead of asking, "Why are they running?" the better question becomes, "Why does their distance ignite so much in me?"

When you can sit with that without collapsing or pursuing, the dynamic changes.

Sometimes the runner stops running. Sometimes the chaser stops chasing. And sometimes both realize that what they felt was real, but the timing and emotional readiness were not aligned.

The dynamic softens when neither side is trying to win.

It dissolves when both can stand on their own, without needing the other to regulate their emotional state.

That is when the connection either evolves… or completes.

Sometimes what we call a "twin flame connection" is not spiritual expansion.

It is spiritual bypassing.

Bypassing does not mean the connection is fake. It means we are using spiritual language to avoid emotional work.

When a connection feels intense, magnetic, and destabilizing, it is tempting to elevate it immediately. We say it is destiny. We say it is divine timing. We say it is karmic. We say it is written in the stars.

And maybe it is.

But sometimes those words become a shield.

Instead of asking why we feel anxious, we say it is a soul contract. Instead of asking why we feel abandoned, we say they are the runner. Instead of asking why we feel unchosen, we say it is part of the mission. Spiritual language can make pain feel meaningful. And meaning is comforting.

But meaning does not replace regulation.

If your body is in constant anxiety, that is not enlightenment. If you are checking your phone every hour, that is not destiny. If you feel powerful only when they are present and collapse when they withdraw, that is not union.

It is an attachment.

Bypassing happens when we use the idea of "higher purpose" to avoid asking grounded questions:

Do I feel safe here? Do I feel chosen here? Do I feel steady here?

It is easier to believe we are in a cosmic test than to admit we are tolerating emotional inconsistency.

I have been there. It is seductive to believe that intensity equals depth. It feels grand. Mythic. Larger than life.

But real spiritual maturity feels different.

It feels calm.

It feels like you can breathe even when the other person is silent. It feels like your life continues expanding whether they text you or not.

When we bypass, we stay suspended in longing. We interpret every small gesture as a sign. We decode breadcrumbs like sacred scripture. We assign spiritual meaning to emotional avoidance.

And we call it awakening.

But awakening without embodiment becomes fantasy.

True awakening integrates both dimensions. You can honor the energetic bond and still ask grounded questions. You can feel the connection, but you still require consistency. You can believe in soul contracts and still refuse emotional instability.

The twin flame narrative becomes unhealthy when it excuses behavior that would otherwise feel unacceptable.

Spiritual bypassing keeps the illusion alive.

Decoding brings you back to yourself.

When you return to your body, your nervous system, your boundaries, your dignity, something interesting happens. The story becomes less dramatic. The connection either stabilizes... or loses its charge.

And that is the real test.

Not whether the bond feels cosmic.

But whether it makes you more whole.

The Difference Between Chemistry and Alignment

Chemistry is immediate. It is the spark in the room. The eye contact that lingers a second too long. The electricity in your skin when they sit too close. It feels alive, magnetic, almost fated. Your body reacts before your mind has time to process it.

In contrast, alignment is quieter.

Chemistry makes your heart race. Alignment makes your nervous system settle.

Chemistry pulls you forward. Alignment holds you steady.

In twin flame dynamics, chemistry is often overwhelming. It can feel otherworldly. Conversations stretch for hours. Silence feels charged. Even conflict feels meaningful. There is an intensity that convinces you something extraordinary is happening.

And sometimes it is.

But intensity alone does not equal compatibility.

Chemistry can exist between two wounded parts that recognize each other. It can exist between two people who activate each other's attachment systems. It can even exist between two people who are not meant to build a life together.

Alignment is different. Alignment reveals itself over time. It shows up in consistency. In how conflicts are handled. Whether both people move toward each other when things become uncomfortable, instead of one advancing while the other retreats.

Chemistry feels like fire. Alignment feels like ground.

Chemistry can make you feel high. Alignment makes you feel safe.

In many twin flame stories, the fire is so powerful that it is mistaken for destiny. The push-pull dynamic feels spiritual. The longing feels sacred. The separation feels like part of a larger mission.

But when you carefully decode the dynamic, you begin to notice something important: Does this connection expand you in real life, or only in imagination?

Alignment does not require you to shrink. It does not require you to decode mixed signals. It does not require you to spiritualize silence. When alignment is present, there is movement. There is mutual effort. There is emotional reciprocity.

Chemistry can make you obsessed.

Alignment makes you secure.

And here is the subtle truth most people avoid: you can have chemistry without alignment. You can even have a profound spiritual connection without practical compatibility.

That does not make the experience meaningless. It simply means the lesson may not be about the union. It may be about self-recognition.

The twin flame dynamic becomes transformative when you can tell the difference between the fire that excites you and the ground that supports you.

Both feel powerful. But only one builds something sustainable.

The decoding begins the moment you ask yourself honestly: when I am with this person, do I feel activated… or anchored?

That question changes everything.

Chapter 8

When the Energy Is Real but the Behavior Doesn't Match

There is a moment in this dynamic when the intensity no longer confuses you; the inconsistency does.

At first, the pull is everything. It overrides logic. It overrides timing. It overrides common sense. You feel something ancient, something familiar, something that does not need proof. The connection feels undeniable, and because it feels undeniable, you assume the rest will align around it.

But then, gradually, something strange begins to happen.

The energy remains strong. The resonance does not fade. The moments together still feel magnetic, almost suspended in time. You laugh differently. You breathe differently. Silence feels full instead of empty. When you are near each other, it feels like recognition.

And yet… outside of those moments, the behavior shifts.

Messages slow down. Plans feel tentative. Warmth turns neutral. What felt expansive suddenly feels restrained. You begin to notice a gap between what you feel and what you show.

This is the part that unsettles you.

Because if the energy were false, it would be easier. You could dismiss it. You could categorize it as fantasy or projection and move on. But that is not what is happening. The energy feels real. The body responds. The heart knows.

What doesn't match is the follow-through.

You start asking quiet questions you don't want to admit out loud. If it's real, why doesn't it stabilize? If it's mutual, why does it retreat? If we both feel this, why does it only expand in certain moments and disappear in others?

At least that's what I experienced.

I remember recognizing the energy clearly: it wasn't imagined. It wasn't forced. It was calm and electric at the same time. But the behavior around it didn't always reflect that depth. And instead of doubting the energy, I began doubting myself.

Maybe I misread it. Maybe I amplified it. Maybe I wanted it more than the other person did. That internal questioning is where many people get lost.

Because this stage is not about whether the connection exists. It is about whether the two nervous systems involved can hold it simultaneously.

Intensity does not automatically translate into readiness. Recognition does not automatically translate into capacity. Two people can feel something profound and still respond to it differently.

One may lean in. The other may freeze. One may speak. The other may retreat into silence.

The energy remains intact, but the expression becomes uneven.

And this unevenness can feel destabilizing, not because the connection is fake, but because it is not mirrored in consistent action.

This is where decoding becomes essential.

Not decoding the other person's feelings. Not decoding hidden messages. But decoding the dynamic itself.

There is a difference between shared intensity and shared stability.

Shared intensity creates sparks. Shared stability creates continuity.

And sometimes, the first arrives before the second, introducing both excitement and uncertainty.

The hardest part of this phase is learning to hold both truths at once: the connection can be real, and the behavior can still be misaligned.

That realization doesn't invalidate what you felt. It simply invites you to see it more clearly.

And clarity is not the end of magic.

It is the beginning of maturity within it.

Why Intensity Can Trigger Opposite Responses

What most people don't talk about is this: the same intensity that feels like coming home to one person can feel like exposure to another.

When a connection carries depth, it doesn't just activate romance. It activates history. It touches old attachment patterns, old fears of loss, old memories of being seen too much or not enough. It surfaces the parts of us that are still unintegrated.

So when two people meet, and the energy is strong, they are not only meeting each other. They are meeting their own nervous systems.

One nervous system might interpret intensity as a sign of safety. Another might interpret intensity as risk.

One might feel, "Finally." The other might feel, "This is too much." And neither of them is lying.

This is why you can sit across from someone, feel electricity in the air, feel your body soften, feel time slow down, and then watch that same person pull back the moment things become emotionally explicit.

It's confusing because the energy didn't disappear. It's still there in the room. It's still there in the silence. But something inside them tightens. Intensity is not neutral. It demands expansion.

And expansion requires capacity.

If someone has never learned how to sit inside powerful emotion without losing control, they may instinctively create distance. Not because they don't feel it, but because they do.

This is where people often misinterpret the dynamic.

They assume:
"If they felt what I felt, they would stay."

But that assumes that feeling automatically equals readiness.
It doesn't.

I had to learn that the hard way. I thought recognition meant alignment. I thought if two people touched something that deep, the next step was obvious.

But depth doesn't override conditioning. It exposes it.

Sometimes the person who pulls away is not less connected, they are less regulated. And that difference changes everything.

When Retreat Is Not Rejection

Here is another uncomfortable truth: retreat does not always mean disinterest.

Sometimes retreat is self-protection; other times, it is overwhelm, or it is the body saying, "I don't know how to stay here without losing control." When someone oscillates between warmth and distance, it can feel like emotional whiplash. One moment you are laughing—relaxed, spontaneous, open. The next moment, there is coolness—detachment, restraint, guardedness.

You start questioning your memory. Was the warmth real? Did I imagine it?

But what if both experiences were valid and real?

What if the warmth was an authentic connection, and the distance, in turn, was an authentic fear?

That possibility doesn't excuse inconsistent behavior or mean you must accept breadcrumbs. However, it does change how you interpret what is happening.

There is a difference between someone who doesn't feel and someone who doesn't know how to hold what they feel.

Decoding that difference is subtle.

One drains you. The other destabilizes you.

Drain feels empty. Destabilization feels intense.

You are not confused because there is nothing there. You are confused because there is too much there and it isn't contained.

Temporary Misalignment or Structural Difference?

This is the part where self-honesty becomes essential.

Some misalignment is temporary. It arises when both people are adjusting to the depth of their experiences. With time, communication, and emotional maturity, the nervous systems begin to synchronize.

But some misalignment is structural.

Structural misalignment means one person is oriented toward expansion, and the other is oriented toward preservation. One grows through depth. The other stabilizes through distance.

At first, the difference feels exciting. Opposites create charge. But over time, the difference becomes repetitive.

Patterns reveal themselves.

Warmth. Retreat. Reunion. Distance.

If the cycle never evolves, you are no longer decoding a mystery. You are observing a rhythm.

And rhythms either expand you or exhaust you. The question is not whether the connection is real. The question is whether the dynamic grows.

That distinction changes the entire conversation.

Chapter 9

The Push and Pull — When Chemistry Becomes a Pattern

At first, the push-and-pull feels romantic.

It feels like tension in a movie. Like longing. Like unfinished sentences hanging in the air. You lean in, they lean back. They lean in, you soften. There is movement. There is a spark. There is a charge.

And in the beginning, because of this, it feels alive.

You tell yourself, This is passion. This is depth. This is magnetic. But magnetism and instability can feel very similar in the early stages.

However, the difference only becomes clear later.

Push and pull is not always dramatic. Sometimes it's subtle. One day, there is warmth — longer messages, spontaneous calls, inside jokes that make you feel chosen. The next day, there is neutrality. Short responses. "Ok." Space where there was once energy.

Nothing technically happened. There was no argument. No clear conflict. Just a shift.

And the shift is what activates you.

You begin decoding tone. Timing. Word choice. You replay conversations in your head, trying to identify the moment when the temperature changed.

It's at this point that chemistry begins to turn into a pattern.

Chemistry feels mutual. The pattern feels repetitive.

In a push–pull dynamic, both people are often responding to their own internal triggers rather than each other. When closeness increases, one nervous system relaxes while the other tightens. When distance appears, the dynamic reverses.

This rhythm exists, but it is a rhythm of tension, not of harmony.

One person may feel most alive in pursuit. The other may feel safest when they are not being emotionally claimed. So when the distance appears, attraction heightens. When closeness stabilizes, the energy cools.

From the outside, it looks confusing. From the inside, it feels intoxicating.

Because unpredictability amplifies emotion.

There is research on intermittent reinforcement — how inconsistent rewards create stronger attachment than consistent ones. But you don't need psychology to understand it. You feel it in your body.

When affection is steady, the nervous system rests.

When affection is inconsistent, the nervous system scans for cues.

Scanning feels like intensity. And intensity can be mistaken for depth. This is the part no one warns you about.

Push and pull creates adrenaline. Adrenaline creates attachment. Attachment creates meaning.

But meaning built on adrenaline does not automatically equal alignment.

Sometimes the connection is real. The laughter is real. The warmth is real. The shared moments are undeniable. But the stability never arrives. And without stability, intensity becomes exhausting.

You start noticing something subtle: you feel most bonded in the moments of reunion. After distance. After silence. After emotional withdrawal. The reconnection feels electric — almost sacred.

But if every high requires a withdrawal first, you are not riding chemistry. You are riding a contrast.

And contrast is not the same as compatibility.

The hard question emerges quietly:

Is this expanding me or keeping me activated?

There is nothing wrong with passion. There is nothing wrong with tension. There is nothing wrong with longing. But when longing becomes the primary fuel of the relationship, something deeper needs to be examined.

A healthy connection can contain excitement without destabilization.

It can contain desire without anxiety.

It can contain closeness without triggering escape.

Push and pull only feels romantic when you believe the next phase will be permanent closeness. When you start recognizing that the cycle resets instead of evolves, something shifts inside you.

You don't become cold. You don't become bitter. You become observant.

And observation is the beginning of decoding.

The moment you stop reacting to the pull, you see the pattern clearly. You notice who moves closer when you step back. You notice who softens when you detach. You notice whether the dynamic transforms or simply repeats.

Some connections need the tension to survive. Remove the chase, and the energy disappears.

In contrast, other connections actually stabilize once the chase ends. That is how you tell the difference.

Push and pull is not proof of destiny. It is proof of activation.

The question is: what is being activated?

Your wounds? Your ego? Your growth? Or your future?

When chemistry becomes a pattern, you are not meant to panic. You are meant to witness.

And once you witness it without needing to fix it, something powerful happens.

The pattern loses control over you.

Chapter 10

Trauma Bond or Twin Flame?

This is the question no one wants to ask out loud.

Because if you're in it, the connection feels sacred. It feels rare. It feels almost cosmic. So even suggesting that it could be psychological rather than spiritual can feel insulting.

But decoding requires courage.

A trauma bond and a twin flame connection can feel eerily similar at the surface.

Both are intense. Both feel magnetic. Both feel hard to let go of. Both can create obsession.

The difference is not in the intensity. The difference is in what the intensity is doing to you.

A trauma bond forms through inconsistency, emotional highs and lows, withdrawal, and then reward. It wires the nervous system into craving the person who destabilizes it. The brain confuses relief with love.

When someone pulls away and then returns, your body experiences a surge of dopamine and cortisol. The reunion feels euphoric. Not because the connection is divine but because your nervous system just exited survival mode.

Relief can feel like destiny.

And that is where many people get lost.

A twin flame connection, if we strip it of fantasy and mythology, is not meant to keep you in survival mode. It may awaken you. It may confront you. It may disrupt you. But at its core, it expands you.

A trauma bond contracts you.

You shrink to maintain it. You overanalyze. You walk on emotional eggshells. You wait for the next text like oxygen.

In a trauma bond, your body feels anxious when they leave and relieved when they return. In a true expanding connection, your body may miss them, but it does not collapse without them.

There is a difference between missing someone and losing yourself.

Sometimes what people call "runner–chaser dynamic" is simply one nervous system that cannot tolerate intimacy and another that cannot tolerate abandonment. That doesn't make it spiritual. It makes it unhealed.

And yet here is the nuance.

Some connections awaken old wounds precisely so they can surface. You meet someone who feels familiar, and suddenly your deepest fears are activated. Not because they are your tormentor, but because they mirror what still needs integration.

So how do you tell the difference?

You don't ask, "Is this intense? You ask, "Am I becoming more whole?" After the storms, do you feel stronger or more dependent? After the silence, do you feel grounded or destabilized? Over time, are you expanding into your own life, or are you orbiting theirs?

A twin flame dynamic, if real, should not require you to abandon your dignity. It should not require you to compete with their indifference. It should not require you to shrink so they don't run.

Intensity alone is not sacred.

Sometimes intensity is just chemistry colliding with unresolved attachment patterns.

And here's the connecting thread you may not expect: It can be both.

A connection, then, can feel spiritually significant and still contain trauma bonding patterns. One does not cancel the other. But one must be healed for the other to stabilize.

If the connection only survives when someone is chasing, it is not a union. It is activation.

If the connection survives even when both step back, breathe, and live their lives, then something deeper is present.

The real test is simple, but uncomfortable:

If this person disappeared tomorrow, would you feel broken or would you feel heartbroken but intact?

Twin flame mythology often glorifies suffering. It romanticizes longing. It tells you that pain is proof.

But pain is not proof of destiny. Pain is proof that something is being touched.

The decoding is not about dismissing your experience. It is about asking whether the connection is building you or keeping you addicted to the high of almost.

Because the truth is, a true spiritual connection does not weaken you. It strengthens your center.

And if you are honest, your body already knows which one this is.

Chapter 11

Obsession, Activation, or Awakening?

It doesn't begin softly.

It begins with a surge.

One day, you are fine. Functional. Living your life. And then something shifts. A glance, a silence, a moment that shouldn't mean much, and suddenly your nervous system is no longer neutral. Your thoughts return to one person without permission. Your chest feels heavier. Or lighter. Or electric. You replay conversations as if there was something hidden inside them that only you can decode.

And the strangest part?

You don't feel weak.

You feel alive.

That's what makes it confusing.

Obsession feels desperate. Activation feels powerful. Awakening feels sacred. But in the body, they can feel almost identical.

I remember telling myself that what I was feeling wasn't attachment. It felt too expensive to be an attachment. It felt like something ancient had been switched on inside me, like a dormant current suddenly running again. I wasn't trying to own anyone. I wasn't afraid of losing them. I simply felt intensely awake.

And intensity, when you are not used to it, can feel like destiny.

This is where decoding matters.

Because intensity alone does not mean alignment.

Obsession narrows you. It contracts your world around one person. Your mood depends on their response. Your stability depends on their availability. Without them, you feel smaller.

Activation expands you. It makes you more creative, more self-aware, more alive, even when they are not present. You feel lit from within.

Awakening destabilizes you at first, but not because of them. It destabilizes you because you are seeing yourself clearly for the first time. Your patterns rise. Your old fears surface. Your hunger for validation becomes visible. Your attachment to intensity reveals itself.

All three can overlap. That overlap is what people often label "twin flame."

But this book is not here to romanticize intensity. It is here to refine it.
The real question is not:
"Are they my twin flame?"
The real question is:
"What is this connection activating inside me?"

If it activates fear of abandonment, that is something to meet.

If it activates a craving to be chosen, that is something to understand.

If it activates expansion, clarity, creativity, and self-respect, that is something to honor.

Activation without awareness becomes obsession. Activation with awareness becomes awakening.

The intensity itself is not the danger.

Unexamined intensity is.

And clarity does not remove the fire.

It teaches you how to hold it without burning yourself.
55

Chapter 12

The Illusion of "The One"

There is a moment in almost every intense connection when you become convinced you have found "the one." It does not arrive as logic. It arrives as knowing. It arrives quietly, like something ancient inside you just nodded in recognition.

At least, that is how it felt to me.

It was not fireworks. It was not an obsession at first. It was a shift in the atmosphere of my own body. The air felt different. Time moved differently. Even ordinary conversations seemed layered, as if something else was happening underneath the words. I remember thinking, " This feels familiar in a way that has nothing to do with memory.

That is the part most people struggle to explain.

When we say "the one," what are we actually describing? Is it destiny? Is it a projection? Is it the sudden expansion of our nervous system because someone mirrors us so precisely that we feel exposed and alive at the same time?

Intensity can feel like fate because it interrupts the ordinary version of us. It makes us aware of ourselves in a heightened way. You notice how you laugh. You notice how you sit. You notice how you breathe when they look at you. You become aware of yourself as if you are both inside your body and slightly outside of it.

That heightened awareness is powerful. It can feel spiritual. It can feel cosmic. It can feel like a thread pulling you toward something inevitable.

But here is what most people do not pause to consider: sometimes what feels like "the one" is not about the other person at all. It is about the part of you that just woke up.

When someone deeply activates you, they do not just enter your life; they disrupt your identity. They challenge the version of yourself that was comfortable, independent, detached, or distracted. They bring forward desire, longing, vulnerability, and even fear. They expose the places where you have been guarded.

And that exposure feels like significance.

This is where the illusion can begin—not because the connection is false, but because we confuse activation with permanence. We assume that the depth of feeling guarantees the outcome. We assume that recognition must lead to union. We assume that 'intensity' must mean 'alignment'.

But intensity can also mean contrast.

It can mean that you have touched something unfinished inside yourself. I learned that the feeling of "the one" is less about ownership and more about revelation. It reveals what you are capable of feeling when your defenses are lowered. It reveals how alive you can become in the presence of someone who reflects your depth back to you. It reveals your hunger for expansion.

And here is the subtle layer most people miss: sometimes we are not drawn to "the one" because they complete us. We are drawn to them because they confront us with who we are becoming.

That confrontation can feel like destiny. It can also feel destabilizing.

Decoding this stage requires honesty. Not cynicism. Not romantic fantasy. Honesty.

When you believe you have found "the one," ask yourself gently: What part of me came alive in their presence? What part of me felt seen? And what part of me felt threatened?

Because the answer is not about them.

It is about you.

And the moment you begin to see that clearly, the dynamic shifts. You are no longer clinging to a person. You are observing a transformation. That is where real decoding begins.

And the moment you begin to see that clearly, the dynamic shifts. You are no longer clinging to a person. You are observing a transformation. That is where real decoding begins.

And there is a moment in every intense connection where you stop asking, "Do they feel it too?" and begin asking something much quieter: "What is this doing to me?"

At first, the focus is always outward. You replay conversations. You analyze their tone. You measure the distance between messages. You interpret silence as a signal. The other person becomes the center of gravity.

But if you look closely, something else is happening beneath that surface.

Your body changes. Your thoughts sharpen. Your emotions amplify. You become hyper-aware not just of them, but of yourself. What you tolerate. What you fear. What you desire but never admit.

The connection feels like it is about the other person. Yet the deeper shift is internal.

Not every intense connection is destiny. And not every activation is obsession. Sometimes what feels cosmic is simply the psyche surfacing material that was dormant. Old attachment patterns. Unmet needs. Forgotten confidence. Unclaimed power.

The mirror does not ask whether the connection is "real." It asks: What part of you came alive?

Did you feel more magnetic? More vulnerable? More anxious? More certain? More afraid of losing something you never fully had?

The dynamic itself is neutral. It amplifies whatever is already inside you. And this is the uncomfortable truth most people skip: if the connection destabilizes you more than it strengthens you, the mirror is not showing romance. It is showing your nervous system.

But if it expands you if you become clearer, steadier, more sovereign, then something else is unfolding.

Decoding is not about labeling the connection too early. It is about observing your own transformation without fantasy and without denial. The twin flame dynamic, real or projected, serves as an accelerator. It reveals what you have been avoiding. It magnifies what you have suppressed. It intensifies what you secretly crave.

The mirror does not lie. But it also does not flatter.

And if you are reading this, you already know something is being reflected back to you. The question is not whether the connection is powerful.

The question is what it is asking you to see.

Chapter 13

When Your Body Knows Before Your Mind Does

Most people think twin flame recognition happens in the mind.
It doesn't.

It happens in the body.

Before you had language for it, before you searched the internet for definitions, before you called it destiny or trauma or karma, your nervous system reacted.

Maybe your chest tightened. Maybe your stomach flipped. Maybe you couldn't sleep after meeting them, or maybe you felt calm in a way that made no sense.

The body registers intensity long before the mind creates meaning.

And this is where decoding becomes honest.

Because not every strong reaction is spiritual. Sometimes it is chemistry. Sometimes it is familiarity. Sometimes it is attachment recognition, your system recognizing a pattern it has known before.

And sometimes… it is expansion.

The difference is subtle.

Attachment feels urgent. Expansion feels powerful.

Attachment makes you lean forward. Expansion lets you stand still.

Attachment scans for danger. Are they pulling away? Did I say something wrong? Expansion feels grounded even in silence.

This is where many people confuse obsession with awakening.

The body in attachment is activated but unstable. There is adrenaline. There is hyper-focus. There is a sense that something must be secured.

The body in awakening feels different. There may still be intensity, but underneath it is steadiness. Even when you miss them, you don't lose yourself. Even when you desire them, you don't shrink.

That distinction matters because if your body feels constantly dysregulated around the connection, that is not cosmic fate. That is a signal.

And decoding requires courage to read signals without romanticizing them.

I once believed intensity alone meant significance. If it shook me, I assumed it was sacred. But over time, I began to notice something: the connections that truly expanded me did not make me smaller.

They did not force me into anxiety. They did not demand I abandon my center.

They awakened me, but they did not destabilize me.

This is the layer most people skip. They go straight to labels. Twin flame. Runner. Chaser. Divine timing.

But before any label, there is your body. Your breath. Your sleep. Your appetite. Your focus. Your sense of self.

Decode there first because the mind can create stories. The body only registers truth.

Chapter 14

The Intensity

There is a moment in almost every intense connection when you become convinced you have found "the one." It does not arrive as logic. It arrives as knowing. It arrives quietly, like something ancient inside you just nodded in recognition.

At least, that is how it felt to me.

It was not fireworks. It was not an obsession at first. It was a shift in the atmosphere of my own body. The air felt different. Time moved differently. Even ordinary conversations seemed layered, as if something else was happening underneath the words. I remember thinking, " This feels familiar in a way that has nothing to do with memory.

That is the part most people struggle to explain.

When we say "the one," what are we actually describing? Is it destiny? Is it a projection? Is it the sudden expansion of our nervous system because someone mirrors us so precisely that we feel exposed and alive at the same time?

Intensity can feel like fate because it interrupts the ordinary version of us. It makes us aware of ourselves in a heightened way. You notice how you laugh. You notice how you sit. You notice how you breathe when they look at you. You become aware of yourself as if you are both inside your body and slightly outside of it.

That heightened awareness is powerful. It can feel spiritual. It can feel cosmic. It can feel like a thread pulling you toward something inevitable.

But here's what many overlook: sometimes, what feels like "the one" is not about them at all; it's about the part of you that just awakened.

When someone deeply activates you, they do not just enter your life. They disrupt your identity. They challenge the version of yourself that was comfortable, independent, detached, or distracted. They bring forward desire, longing, vulnerability, and even fear. They expose the places where you have been guarded.

And that exposure feels like significance.

This is where the illusion can begin not because the connection is false, but because we confuse activation with permanence. We assume that the depth of feeling guarantees the outcome. We assume that recognition must lead to union. We assume that 'intensity' must mean 'alignment'.
But intensity can also mean contrast.

It can mean that you have touched something unfinished inside yourself. I learned that the feeling of "the one" is less about ownership and more about revelation. It reveals what you are capable of feeling when your defenses are lowered. It reveals how alive you can become in the presence of someone who reflects your depth back to you. It reveals your hunger for expansion.

And here is the subtle layer most people miss: sometimes we are not drawn to "the one" because they complete us. We are drawn to them because they confront us with who we are becoming.

That confrontation can feel like destiny. It can also feel destabilizing.

Decoding this stage requires honesty. Not cynicism. Not romantic fantasy. Honesty.

When you believe you have found "the one," ask yourself gently: What part of me came alive in their presence? What part of me felt seen? And what part of me felt threatened?

Because the answer is not about them.

It is about you.

And the moment you begin to see that clearly, the dynamic shifts. You are no longer clinging to a person. You are observing a transformation.

That is where real decoding begins.

Chapter 15

The Silence Between You

No one prepares you for the silence.

Not the dramatic ending. Not the explosive fight. Just the space that slowly stretches between two people who once felt electrically connected. The conversations become shorter. The pauses last longer. You reread messages that once felt alive and wonder what changed.

Silence is rarely neutral inside a twin flame dynamic. It feels loaded. It feels intentional. Even when nothing is said, something feels like it is happening.

At least, that is how it felt for me.

When the silence came, I did not immediately panic. I observed it. But observation does not mean detachment. There is a subtle shift that happens inside your body when someone who once felt close becomes distant. Your mind begins searching for meaning. Did I say something wrong? Did they lose interest? Is this a test? Is this destiny rearranging itself?

The silence becomes a mirror.

If you are anxious, it activates your fear of abandonment. If you are avoidant, it feels like relief. If you are deeply attached, it feels like being suspended in the air with no ground beneath you.

The problem is not the silence itself. The problem is what the silence awakens inside you.

When two people are steady, silence can feel peaceful. It can feel like space. But when a connection is intense, silence feels like withdrawal.

The nervous system does not know whether to relax or prepare for loss. This is where decoding becomes necessary.

Is the silence a manipulation? Is it emotional immaturity? Is it two people needing space? Or is it simply two nervous systems trying to regulate in different ways?

You cannot answer that by staring at your phone. You answer it by noticing your own reaction.

If silence feels unbearable, that is information. If silence makes you feel powerful and grounded, that is information too. If silence makes you fantasize about reunion, that is also data.

Twin flame language often romanticizes separation as part of the journey. But not every silence is spiritual. Sometimes it is simply avoidance. Sometimes it is incompatibility. Sometimes it is growth. And sometimes it is just two people unsure of how to hold intensity without destabilizing themselves.

Silence does not automatically mean fate is working behind the scenes. Sometimes silence is just silence.

But what it reveals about you is where the real decoding begins.

When you stop trying to control the gap and start studying your own internal shift, the power returns to you. You realize the connection is not only between two bodies. It is between your nervous system and your expectations.

And once you see that clearly, silence loses its drama.

It becomes information.

Chapter 16

The Fantasy Version of Them

There is always a version of them that lives inside your head.

It is not the version that delays replies. Not the one who says, "We are just friends." Not the one who pulls away when things become too intimate.

It is the version who looked at you that first night. The version that held your hand a little longer than necessary. The version that made you feel seen in a way that felt almost supernatural.

That version becomes sacred.

And slowly, without noticing, you begin relating more to that inner version than to the real human standing in front of you. This shift is subtle, yet profound, as your focus drifts from reality to memory.

It's at this crucial point that decoding becomes delicate.

This fantasy version, importantly, is not a lie. It is built from real moments. Real warmth. Real chemistry. Real connection. Yet, it remains incomplete: a highlight reel extracted from intensity.

When connection activates something deep inside you, your mind wants to preserve it. So it edits. It remembers selectively. It protects the feeling by polishing the memory.

At least that is what I noticed in myself.

I was not imagining someone entirely different. I was remembering the best version of her. The one who was warm, open, and curious. The one who felt like she was transmitting something through her eyes. That version felt eternal.

While I cherished that memory, I had to remember: humans are not eternal versions. They fluctuate.

The fantasy begins when you start waiting for the highlight to return instead of evaluating the present reality. You tell yourself, "She is just overwhelmed." Or "He is just scared." Or "This intensity needs time."

There are moments when this hopeful narrative reflects reality.

But sometimes you are in love with the activation, not the actual person. That is a difficult sentence to read when you are inside it.

Because the activation feels sacred. It feels cosmic. It feels destined. And maybe it is. But destiny does not remove discernment.

The fantasy version keeps the dynamic alive long after the present version has cooled. It makes you tolerant of inconsistency because you believe you have seen something deeper. You convince yourself that the deeper layer is the "real" one, and the current behavior is temporary.

But what if both are real?

What if the warmth was real, and the withdrawal is also real?

Decoding does not ask you to destroy the magic. It asks you to hold both truths at once. The person who activated you exists. And the person who pulls away exists. The question is not which one is true.

The question is which one is consistent.

Fantasy keeps you suspended in potential. Reality shows you a pattern.

And patterns, not sparks, determine whether something can grow.

When you begin to separate the activation from the actual person, you do not lose the magic. You regain clarity. You stop chasing the highlight and start observing the whole picture.

And that is where maturity begins inside the twin flame dynamic.

Chapter 17

The Pattern You Keep Calling Fate

At some point, you start noticing something uncomfortable.

You notice something uncomfortable. It's not just that they pull away, but that this happens in the same way, at the same stage, and after the same kind of intimacy.

At first, the experience feels mysterious. The second time, confusion sets in. By the third time, it feels familiar. Instead of calling this a pattern, though, you might label it as timing, fear, or divine orchestration.

For a long time, I reframed the cycle: "This is just how twin flames move," I told myself. Assigning spiritual language felt lighter than calling it repetition.

There is always a moment in this dynamic when everything feels aligned. You laugh. You share. You touch. You remember why this connection feels different from anyone else. And just when the ground begins to feel solid, something shifts.

Distance creeps in.

Not dramatically. Not with a fight. Just a subtle withdrawal. A cooler tone. A slower reply. A slight wall where warmth used to be. And the strange part? You almost expect it. That is when you know you are inside a pattern.

Patterns feel mystical when you don't name them. They feel predictable when you do.

This is not about blaming the other person. It is about observing the rhythm. Every dynamic has a rhythm. Some move toward closeness and stabilize. Others move toward closeness and retreat.

If closeness is consistently followed by distance, that is not fate. That is wiring.

Sometimes it is their wiring. Sometimes it is yours. Sometimes it is the chemistry between two nervous systems that were activated at the same time but calibrated differently.

The mind will always try to spiritualize repetition because repetition with meaning feels better than repetition without growth.

But decoding requires honesty.

If every reunion is followed by separation, and every intimacy is followed by withdrawal, then you are not in a mystery. You are in a loop.

The loop does not mean the connection is fake. It means the dynamic is unresolved.

You can have something sacred and still be stuck in a cycle. And here is the part most people avoid:

If you already know the pattern, and you still enter it again, then the pattern is not only happening to you. It is happening through you.

That realization is not meant to shame you. It is meant to empower you.

Because fate cannot be changed. Patterns can.

When you start seeing the rhythm clearly, something shifts. You stop reacting in surprise. You stop romanticizing the withdrawal. You stop interpreting distance as depth.

You begin asking a different question.

Not, "Why are they doing this?"

But, "Why does this rhythm still feel familiar to me?"

That is where decoding turns inward.

And that is where the twin flame story stops being about them and starts revealing you.

Chapter 18

Why Calm Feels Boring After Intensity

There is a moment in every intense connection when something changes. The fire that once felt overwhelming begins to soften. The constant thinking slows down. The emotional spikes aren't as sharp. And instead of relief, many people feel something unexpected.

They feel… bored.

It's rarely admitted out loud, because boredom sounds like disinterest. It sounds like the connection is fading. But what is actually happening is far more subtle. When you've grown used to intensity as proof of meaning, calm can feel like absence.

Intensity is loud. It demands attention. It pulls your focus into the body. It creates adrenaline, anticipation, longing, fear of loss, and excitement. It keeps you alert. It keeps you scanning. It keeps you engaged.

Calm does none of that.

Calm does not chase you. It does not spike your nervous system. It does not create emotional drama that you have to decode at midnight. Calm simply exists. And if your body has been trained to equate intensity with importance, calm can feel like something is missing.

At least, that's what I noticed in myself.

There were moments when the energy between us was quiet. No push. No pull. No dramatic story running in my head. Just presence. And instead of relaxing into it, I found myself wondering, "Where did the spark go?" As if peace needed to jus

That question alone reveals the pattern.

When intensity becomes familiar, the nervous system begins to crave it. Not because it is healthy, but because it is recognizable. The highs and lows create movement. They create a storyline. They make the connection feel alive.

Calm feels still.

And stillness can feel like emptiness if you are not used to it.

This is where many twin flame dynamics become confusing. The connection may still be there. The resonance may still exist. But without the emotional spikes, the mind starts to doubt. It asks, "Is this it? Is this all?" As if love must always be dramatic to be real.

But what if calm is not the end of the spark?

What if calm is the next stage of it?

It is easy to bond through chaos. It is harder to stay present without it.

When the nervous system is no longer activated by fear of losing the other person, the body relaxes. When you are no longer trying to prove, chase, or secure the connection, the energy stabilizes. That stability can feel unfamiliar because it requires no effort.

And effort is often mistaken for depth.

It is easy to bond through chaos. It is harder to stay present without it.

This is why some people unconsciously create small disruptions when things become steady. A delayed reply. A subtle withdrawal. A sudden distance. Not always intentionally. Sometimes it is simply the body trying to recreate the familiar voltage of intensity.

Because calm does not give you the same rush.

But calm gives you something else.

It gives you clarity.

When intensity fades, you can finally see what remains without distortion. You can ask yourself whether you feel grounded or just stimulated. Whether you feel safe or just activated. Whether you feel expanded or just consumed.

Intensity is exciting.

Calm is revealing.

And the truth is, many people say they want peace, but their nervous system is still addicted to fire.

Decoding this is not about judging the intensity. It is about recognizing what your body has learned to crave. If calm feels boring, it may not be because the connection is weak. It may be because your system has only learned how to recognize love when it is loud.

The deeper question becomes this:

Can you stay when it is quiet?

Not because the other person is pulling you.

Not because the drama keeps you hooked, but because the connection stands without needing to prove itself.

That is where decoding truly begins.

Chapter 19

When You Stop Trying to Be Chosen

There is a quiet shift that happens long before the connection ends.

It does not look dramatic. It does not require a confrontation. It does not even require distance.

It happens inside you.

For a long time, whether you admit it or not, a part of you wants to be chosen. Chosen over the doubt. Chosen over the distance. Chosen over other people. Chosen clearly and without ambiguity.

You may call it love. You may call it destiny. You may call it divine timing. But underneath all of it is something very human: the desire to be claimed without hesitation.

That desire is not weakness. It is natural.

But when the twin flame dynamic becomes unsteady, the need to be chosen can quietly take over your energy. You start measuring your worth against their consistency. You interpret their warmth as validation and their withdrawal as rejection. Even if you say you are detached, your nervous system still scans for confirmation.

And then something changes.

You get tired.

Not tired of loving. Not tired of the connection. Just tired of leaning forward.

You notice that your energy has been subtly angled toward them for months, maybe years. You realize that you have been waiting not passively, but energetically, for them to step fully in.

And one day, you straighten your posture.

You stop trying to prove your depth. You stop trying to decode every silence. You stop adjusting yourself to feel more compatible.

You do not withdraw in anger. You do not leave dramatically. You simply return your energy to yourself. That is the moment the dynamic shifts. Because when you stop trying to be chosen, you start choosing.

You choose how you respond. You choose how much effort you give. You choose whether you participate in the loop again.

And here is the paradox: when you no longer need them to choose you, you become more magnetic. Not because you are playing a game, but because your energy is no longer stretched outward.

This is not detachment as defense. It is detachment as sovereignty.

The connection may still exist. The chemistry may still spark. The memories may still feel sacred. But you are no longer bargaining with your self-worth inside it.

You do not need them to validate the experience you had.

You lived it.

You felt it.

You know it was real.

And because you know that, you no longer need proof.

When you reach this point, something subtle but profound happens: the twin flame dynamic stops being about union and starts being about integration.

You are not waiting anymore.

You are standing.

And from that stance, everything looks different.

Chapter 20

Integration: When the Energy Comes Back to You

There is a stage in every intense connection that feels quieter than obsession and steadier than detachment. It does not announce itself. It does not feel like triumph. It feels like something is settling.

This is integration.

Integration is not forgetting them. It is not pretending that the connection was exaggerated. It is not forcing yourself to move on. It is something much more subtle.

It is when the energy you once directed toward them returns to you.

At first, your thoughts circled them constantly. Your body reacted to their presence. Your mood shifted with their attention. Your imagination filled in the silence. The connection occupied space in your nervous system.

But over time, especially if you have been decoding honestly, something shifts. You begin to notice that your thoughts are not consumed. You can remember them without spiraling. You can feel warmth without urgency. You can experience attraction without losing your footing.

The energy is still there.

But it is not pulling you forward.

It is sitting inside you.

That is integration.

Integration means the activation has been absorbed. The lesson is no longer external. The intensity has been processed. You are no longer waiting for the next message to regulate your state. You are no longer measuring your value by their consistency.

You still care.

But you are not tilted.

This is the stage where many people feel confused because it does not look dramatic enough to be significant. There are no fireworks. No declarations. No endings that close a chapter loudly.

Instead, there is clarity.

You realize the connection changed you. It opened something. It exposed something. It awakened something. And now that something belongs to you.

Not to the dynamic.

Integration means the activation has been absorbed. The lesson is no longer external. The intensity has been processed. You are no longer waiting for the next message to regulate your state. You are no longer measuring your value by their consistency.

You still care.

But you are not tilted.

This is the stage where many people feel confused because it does not look dramatic enough to be significant. There are no fireworks. No declarations. No endings that close a chapter loudly.

Instead, there is clarity.

You realize the connection changed you. It opened something. It exposed something. It awakened something. And now that something belongs to you.

Not to the dynamic.

Chapter 21

Love Without Collapse

For a long time, I believed love was supposed to dismantle me.

Not completely. Not destructively. But enough that I could feel it in my bones. Enough to rearrange my thinking, disturb my sleep, shift my center of gravity.

If it didn't move me, I questioned it.

If it didn't destabilize me, I doubted it.

Intensity felt like proof.

But collapse is not proof of love. It is proof of impact.

And impact alone does not determine alignment.

There is a version of love that does not require you to shrink, to chase, to overextend, or to silently brace yourself for withdrawal. There is a version of love that does not feel like standing on unstable ground, waiting to see whether the floor will hold.

It feels steady.

And for someone used to intensity, steady can feel unfamiliar.

Love without collapse does not remove chemistry. It does not remove depth. It does not remove magnetism. It simply removes fear as the engine.

You love from wholeness, not from hunger.

You do not need to perform to keep it. You do not need to decode every pause. You do not need to tilt your energy forward, hoping to be chosen. You stand upright.

This does not mean the twin flame dynamic was meaningless. It may have been the doorway. It may have been the ignition. It may have been the mirror that forced you to see yourself clearly.

But ignition is not the same as endurance.

Love without collapse feels different in the body. The nervous system does not spike and crash. It does not swing between euphoria and panic. It breathes. It rests. It expands gradually instead of exploding.

It may not feel cinematic.

But it feels sustainable.

And perhaps that is the deeper evolution of this entire decoding process. Not to prove whether someone is your twin flame.

Not to secure a union.

Not to justify intensity.

But to learn how to love without abandoning yourself.

Because once you can do that, the dynamic changes automatically.

You are no longer pulled by unpredictability. You are no longer addicted to emotional voltage. You are no longer mistaking instability for destiny. It is more powerful.

You can love deeply and remain centered. You can feel chemistry and remain sovereign. You can choose a connection without collapsing into it.
That is no less romantic.

And when you reach that point, whether the person stays, leaves, returns, or transforms, you remain intact.

Not guarded.

Not numb.

Whole.

Chapter 22

Trauma Bond or Sacred Bond?

There is a question that many people are afraid to ask once they have labeled something a twin flame.

What if this is not sacred?

What if this is trauma?

The fear of asking that question is understandable. When a connection has felt cosmic, life-altering, deeply activating, it can feel almost insulting to reduce it to something psychological. Trauma sounds clinical. Sacred sounds divine. One feels heavy. The other feels elevated. But the truth is not threatened by examination.

I once resisted this question myself. The intensity felt too meaningful to be reduced to attachment language. The synchronicities felt too precise. The eye contact felt too charged. It seemed impossible that something that shook me that deeply could simply be pattern recognition inside my nervous system.

But decoding requires courage.

Trauma bonds are built on unpredictability. They are formed when closeness and withdrawal alternate, keeping the nervous system alert. The body begins to associate emotional spikes with significance. The inconsistency strengthens the attachment rather than weakening it.

Sacred bonds feel intense, too, but they do not destabilize your identity.

That is the difference.

A trauma bond keeps you anxious about losing the connection. A sacred bond expands your sense of self, whether the person is present or not.

A trauma bond makes you shrink to preserve closeness. A sacred bond makes you more yourself in their presence. A trauma bond depends on volatility to feel alive. A sacred bond can survive steadiness.

The confusion happens because both can feel magnetic.

Both can feel consuming. Both can feel destined. But the body responds differently over time.

In trauma bonding, the nervous system never fully rests. Even during warm moments, there is underlying tension. You feel relief when they lean in and anxiety when they lean away. The connection becomes regulating and dysregulating at the same time.

In sacred bonding, even during separation, there is stability. You may miss them. You may feel longing. But your core does not feel threatened. You do not feel erased.

The most difficult part of decoding is admitting that sometimes we spiritualize our wounds because it feels more meaningful than calling them wounds.

If someone activates childhood abandonment, we may call it karmic.

If someone triggers our fear of being unseen, we may call it destiny.

If someone oscillates between warmth and distance, we may call it divine timing.

But sacredness does not require suffering to prove itself.

This does not mean every intense connection is trauma; rather, it means you must be honest about what is being activated inside you. Consider this: does the connection expand you, or does it destabilize you?

In addition, do you feel more grounded in yourself or more dependent on their attention? Similarly, do you become clearer or more confused?

Importantly, discovering that trauma was part of the bond carries no shame. Trauma explains the pull; it does not invalidate the magic.

At the same time, sacredness does not erase trauma. Sometimes both are present. A connection can both activate old wounds and awaken new consciousness.

With this understanding, the real decoding is not choosing one label over the other. Instead, it is noticing which one governs your behavior.

If fear governs your decisions, you are not yet in sovereignty.

If clarity governs your decisions, something sacred may be unfolding. You do not have to rush to decide which one it is.

But you must be willing to observe yourself without romantic filters. Because sacred bonds strengthen your center.

Trauma bonds, by contrast, challenge your stability and often create uncertainty and dependency.

And knowing the difference is the beginning of maturity inside the twin flame dynamic.

Chapter 23

Loving Without Ownership

There was a point where I realized something uncomfortable. I did not just love the connection. I wanted to keep it.

Not physically. Not legally. Not officially.

But energetically.

I wanted it to remain mine.

That realization humbled me.

Because love sounds pure, but ownership hides quietly underneath it.

In intense connections, ownership rarely shows up as control. It shows up as a subtle expectation. A belief that because something felt sacred, it should remain accessible. Because something felt profound, it should not drift into ordinary distance.

But love and ownership are not the same.

Ownership wants permanence.

Love wants truth.

Ownership says, "After everything we shared, you cannot disappear."
Love says, "If your path moves, I will still be whole."

Ownership clings to the narrative. It wants the connection to justify its intensity. It wants the story to resolve in a way that makes sense of the suffering.

Love does not require resolution or certainty.

Love is possible without possessing or controlling.

Reaching this stage was one of the hardest parts.

When you release ownership, you release leverage. You stop striving to secure outcomes. You stop interpreting every action. You stop measuring whether you matter enough.

And that can feel like loss at first.

Yet once ownership dissolves, something surprising unfolds.

The connection becomes lighter.

You no longer monitor it. You no longer manage it. You no longer guard it from possible futures.

You allow it to breathe. And when something can breathe, you finally see what it truly is.

For some connections, that freedom deepens the bond. For others, the connection fades or quietly shifts away.

But either way, you remain intact.

Loving without ownership reflects maturity, not detachment. It is the ability to say:

"What we experienced was real. What we shared mattered. But I do not need to cage it to honor it."

That is when twin flame energy stops feeling like a test and starts feeling like a chapter.

And chapters do not need to be owned to be meaningful.

They only need to be lived.

<h1 style="text-align:center">Chapter 24</h1>

<h2 style="text-align:center">The Role of Ego in the Twin Flame Dynamic</h2>

It is easy to speak about the ego as if it belongs only to the other person. The ego runs from depth. The ego avoids vulnerability. The ego fears intimacy. But understanding becomes honest when we recognize that the ego is present on both sides.

The ego does not always look arrogant. Sometimes it looks wounded. Sometimes it looks spiritual. Sometimes it hides inside the idea of being "the awakened one."

I did not see my own ego at first.

I thought I was loving purely. I thought I was patient. I thought I was evolved enough to understand the push and pull. But beneath the language of destiny and divine timing, there was something else operating quietly.

I wanted to be the one who understood the connection more deeply. I wanted to be the one who could see beyond the fear. I wanted to be chosen not just romantically, but spiritually.

That desire is subtle; it can be easy to overlook within sincere intentions, yet it still shapes your motives.

It does not announce itself as pride. Instead, it quietly creates a sense of specialness or importance.

Ego in the twin flame dynamic often attaches itself to identity. "This connection is different." "We are not like other couples." "No one else would understand this."

And sometimes that is true.

But ego turns uniqueness into superiority.

As a result, it begins to measure the connection against ordinary love and concludes that ordinary love is beneath it. Calm feels boring. Stability feels less profound. Mutual availability feels too simple.

The ego prefers intensity because intensity feels exceptional.

However, there is also another layer to consider.

The ego does not like rejection. When the other person withdraws, the ego reacts. It may disguise itself as heartbreak, but beneath it lies humiliation. "How could they not see what this is?" "How could they not recognize what we have?"

The ego does not just want love.

It wants confirmation.

It wants the narrative to be validated.

It wants the spiritual story to be reciprocated.

If you decode honestly, you see ego fuels the chase and withdrawal. It also fuels the belief that the connection must resolve dramatically and that the story must end in union. Anything else, it seems, would diminish its meaning.

But love does not require ego to survive.

The ego needs to be right. But love needs to be true, and that is enough.

The ego wants the story to prove something. Love wants the experience to unfold.

When the ego is strong in the twin flame dynamic, every action is interpreted personally. Silence becomes an insult. Distance becomes rejection. Inconsistency becomes a challenge. The connection becomes a reflection of worth.

When ego softens, something shifts. You stop trying to win the connection. You stop trying to be the more conscious one. You stop needing the story to justify itself.

You can love without needing to conquer.

You can feel a connection without elevating it above all others.

And perhaps the most difficult realization is this:

Sometimes what we call "divine union" is the ego's refusal to accept an incomplete story.

Integration weakens the ego. It does not destroy passion. It removes the need to dominate the narrative.

The twin flame dynamic becomes lighter when the ego is no longer driving it. You stop trying to prove that it is extraordinary. You stop trying to rescue it. You stop trying to align it.

You let it be what it is.

And in that letting, you discover whether what remains is love, or attachment to the identity the connection gave you.

Ego is not the enemy.

It is simply the part of you that wants the story to end the way you imagined.

Decoding it is not about suppressing the ego.

It is about seeing when it is steering.

Chapter 25

Maybe It Was Never About Them

Here is the part most people do not want to hear.

What if the twin flame was never the destination?

What if the obsession, the longing, the magnetism, the push–pull all of it — was not proof of cosmic pairing...

But proof of your own untapped power?

That realization is disruptive.

Because it removes the pedestal.

It suggests that what felt rare may have been a mirror. What felt destined may have been a trigger for an awakening. What felt irreplaceable may have been catalytic.

Of course, I resisted that idea at first.

Because if it was not "about us," then what was it really about?

It was about identity.

Before the connection, you were stable, functional, maybe successful. But something in you was dormant. Then came activation. Suddenly, your creativity sharpened, awareness expanded, and emotional depth intensified.

You became more.

Was that because of them?

Or because something inside you finally broke open?

It is easier to attribute transformation to another person. It feels romantic. It feels mystical.

But what if they did not give you anything?

What if they exposed what was already there?

This is where the twin flame dynamic becomes dangerous.

If you believe they are the source of your expansion, you will unconsciously limit your growth to their presence.

If you believe they are the key, you will wait at the door.

But if you realize they were the trigger, not the source, something radical happens.

You stop needing them to continue evolving.

You stop fearing that losing them means losing the intensity.

You stop believing that no one else could ever meet you at that level. Because you were the level.

They activated it.

That is disruptive.

Because it dismantles the myth that the connection is singularly divine.

It may have been sacred.

But it was not sovereign.

You are.

And once you understand that, you stop asking:

"Are they my twin flame?"

And you start asking:

"Who am I becoming?"

That is where decoding turns into liberation.

Chapter 26

The Freedom to Choose Again

There was a time when I thought this connection defined my path.

It's not because I was dependent on it, but because it felt so rare that I believed it must be central—a once-in-a-lifetime alignment. When something feels that significant, it quietly begins to shape your decisions.

You plan around it. You measure other connections against it. You hold space for it even when it isn't fully present. You don't even realize you're doing it. Until one day you notice something subtle:

You still love, but you are no longer waiting. This realization brings freedom back into your life.

Freedom does not mean the connection disappears. It means it no longer determines your future. It no longer shapes who you can meet, what you can explore, or how far you can expand.

You can remember it without organizing your life around it. You can honor it without reserving your heart indefinitely. That shift is quiet, but powerful.

Every intense dynamic eventually arrives at a crossroads. Not a dramatic one with slamming doors, but one where you look inward and realize: "I am allowed to choose again."

Choose joy. Choose stability. Choose a new energy. Choose a different rhythm.

Even if you choose the same person, do so with clarity, not attachment.

Freedom to choose again is not a betrayal of the connection. It is a graduation from unconscious loyalty.

At each stage, the connection changed: When you were activated, it felt fated. When you were attached, it felt consuming. When you were integrating, it felt instructive.

Now, you can see the connection simply as part of your story.

And stories do not cage you.

You do not have to stay in a dynamic just because it once awakened you. Awakening is not a contract. It is a catalyst.

If the connection evolves, it's beautiful. If it becomes friendship, that's beautiful too. If it dissolves, it's still beautiful. Why? Because now you don't choose from fear of losing something rare.

You are choosing from self-trust.

That is the final decoding.

Twin flame does not mean forever. It means meeting yourself through another. Once you meet yourself, you are free.

Chapter 27

When the Bond Is Real, But the Timing Isn't

There is something rarely said out loud in the twin flame world. The connection can be real, and still not be aligned. Recognition does not automatically mean readiness. Intensity does not automatically mean destiny. Spiritual language can sometimes delay the very discernment that would set you free.

I know how difficult it is to reach this realization. When you are inside the dynamic, it does not feel like a choice. It feels like gravity. It feels like something larger than you. And when friends say, "Just leave," it sounds ignorant. When family says, "You deserve better," it feels dismissive. Because they are not inside the current.

But decoding requires something deeper than validation. It requires honesty.

Does this connection expand you when you are not in contact? Or does it consume your mental space? Does it allow you to live fully in your own rhythm? Or does it quietly keep you suspended between hope and restraint?

A sacred bond can challenge you. It can stretch your ego. It can awaken parts of you that were dormant. But it should not require you to shrink your world around it. It should not demand indefinite waiting. It should not reduce your life to "when" instead of "now."

And here is the disruptive truth: if continuing your expansion weakens the bond, then the bond was not as sacred as you believed. A real connection does not collapse because you chose yourself.

This is not about walking away. It is about standing upright.

Chapter 28

Loving Without Losing Yourself

There was a time when loving someone felt like surrender. Not the romantic kind of surrender, but the kind where your thoughts slowly reorganize around the other person. You begin measuring your emotional weather by their tone. You begin adjusting your pace to match their availability. You tell yourself it's devotion, or patience, or spiritual maturity. But quietly, something shifts. You are no longer fully standing in your own center.

This is where many twin flame dynamics become confusing. The connection feels expansive, yet your daily life feels smaller. You feel awakened, yet distracted. You feel deeply seen, yet subtly destabilized.

It took me time to understand that love and collapse can feel similar in the beginning. Both soften you. Both make you vulnerable. Both expose your ego. But one strengthens your spine over time, and the other weakens it.

Loving without losing yourself requires discipline. Not emotional coldness. Not detachment. Discipline. The discipline to notice when your thoughts are looping. The discipline to continue building your life even when the connection feels magnetic. The discipline to stay in your own rhythm instead of synchronizing entirely to someone else's.

A sacred bond should deepen your self-respect, not erode it. It should increase your clarity, not blur it. It should allow you to say, "I choose this," instead of, "I cannot help this."

When you can love someone and still feel grounded in your own life, your own friendships, your own purpose, then the bond becomes clean. It stops being gravity and starts being presence.

And presence is very different from pull.

Pull feels urgent. Presence feels steady.

Decoding the twin flame dynamic is not about deciding whether the connection is real. It is about deciding whether you remain real inside it.

Chapter 29

The Evolution Beyond the Dynamic

There comes a point in every intense connection where the question quietly changes. It is no longer, "Will we end up together?" It becomes, "Who am I becoming through this?"

That shift is subtle, but it marks the beginning of evolution.

In the early stages, the twin flame dynamic feels like destiny. It feels rare, cosmic, irreplaceable. The energy is loud. The longing is sharp. The recognition is undeniable. But over time, if you allow yourself to grow instead of orbit, something changes. The intensity begins to reorganize. What once felt like fire becomes information.

You see the pattern without drowning in it. You feel the pull without collapsing. You love without losing your own life.

This is where evolution happens. Not when the connection disappears, and not necessarily when it unites. Evolution happens when you stop defining yourself by the dynamic at all.

The twin flame experience may have awakened you. It may have dismantled your ego. It may have exposed your attachment, your longing, your hunger for transcendence. But its highest function was never to trap you in a story. It was to expand your identity.

Some bonds remain romantic. Some transform into friendship. Some dissolve entirely. But the evolution is personal. It does not depend on the other person's readiness. It does not require their agreement. It does not wait for timing.

When you evolve beyond the dynamic, you stop asking whether the bond will survive. You ask whether you have integrated the lesson.

And here is the truth that feels both simple and disruptive: if a connection is truly sacred, it will evolve with you. And if it cannot evolve, then its purpose was activation, not permanence.

Evolution does not mean forgetting. It does not mean denying the intensity. It means you no longer need the intensity to feel alive.

You become steady.

And steadiness is not dull.

It is powerful.

Chapter 30

The Chaser Is Not the Hero

The chaser often believes they are the awakened one. The deeper one. The braver one. The one capable of feeling at a spiritual level that the runner cannot yet access.

But chasing does not automatically equal depth.

Sometimes chasing is not devotion.

It is anxiety presenting itself in a form that feels like a destined connection, even if it may not be.

The chaser feels everything intensely. The pull. The silence. The shifts in tone. The distance. The warmth. The withdrawal. Their nervous system becomes tuned to the other person's frequency. Every interaction carries meaning.

And meaning feels powerful.

But intensity is not proof of alignment.

It is proof of activation.

Chasers often believe they are fighting for love. But if we decode honestly, we see that they are often fighting uncertainty. The unknown is unbearable. The lack of clarity feels destabilizing. So they lean in harder. They pursue. They try to understand. They decode. They seek reassurance.

They call it spiritual persistence.

But persistence can sometimes be the fear of letting go.

The chaser does not chase because they are weak. They chase because they feel something that reorganizes them. That feeling becomes a reference point. And once the reference exists, they want it stabilized.

Here is the dismantling:

The chaser is not always more awake. They are more activated.

Activation creates urgency. Urgency creates movement. Movement looks like devotion. But devotion that destabilizes your own peace is not sacred. It is attachment seeking resolution.

When the chaser stops chasing, something powerful happens. The intensity does not disappear — it reorganizes. The need to interpret every signal fades. The obsession quiets. The nervous system stabilizes. And suddenly, the dynamic changes.

Because the chase was never about the runner alone.

It was about the chaser's relationship with uncertainty.

Once that is integrated, the power equalizes.

Chapter 31

The Runner Is Not a Villain

Most chasers believe the runner is hiding something profound. A secret love. A deeper fear. A suppressed awakening. The runner becomes mystical simply because they are unavailable.

But distance does not automatically equal depth.

Sometimes the runner is not spiritually overwhelmed. Sometimes they are simply uninterested in the intensity you are experiencing. Sometimes they feel affection, attraction, even care, but not the same magnitude of attachment.

And that truth is hard to accept.

It is easier to believe they are terrified of the depth than to consider they may not feel it the same way.

The twin flame narrative often romanticizes avoidance. It turns emotional withdrawal into spiritual polarity. It turns inconsistency into divine timing. It turns mixed signals into soul contracts.

But let's decode this clearly.

If someone repeatedly creates distance, that is information. If someone labels you as "just a friend" more than once, that is information. If someone is warm in person but cold in consistency, that is information. Information is not mystical.

It is data.

And data does not require spiritual translation to be understood.

The runner does not need to be decoded as a cosmic archetype. They need to be seen as a human being operating within their current emotional capacity.

Sometimes they run because they are avoidant. Sometimes they run because they are overwhelmed. Sometimes they run because they do not want the same depth. Sometimes they run because they prefer freedom over fusion.

None of those requires mythology.

The dismantling happens here:

The runner is not your destiny puzzle. They are a person making choices.

And once you see that, the power dynamic shifts.

You stop decoding their silence as sacred. You stop interpreting distance as destiny. You stop assigning spiritual meaning to every inconsistency. You begin asking a more grounded question:

"Does this behavior align with what I want?"

And that question ends the chase.

Chapter 32

Friendship in a Twin Flame Dynamic — Integration or Intermission?

At some point, many intense connections settle into something that looks calmer. The urgency fades. The labels soften. The language becomes safer. "We're just friends" replaces "What are we?" And on the surface, it feels mature. Evolved. Reasonable.

But friendship inside a twin flame dynamic is not automatically neutral. Sometimes it is genuine integration. The intensity has done its work. The nervous systems are no longer reactive. There is no secret negotiation happening beneath every conversation. Two people can meet, laugh, talk, and leave without emotional aftershocks. Here, friendship is evolution, not a downgrade.

But sometimes friendship is a quieter form of attachment.

It becomes the acceptable version of longing. A way to stay connected without addressing the imbalance. One person says "friend," but still hopes. The other says "friend," but still pulls when it feels too close. Nothing dramatic happens, yet something subtle remains unresolved.

This is where decoding becomes important.

Ask yourself gently: when you see them as a friend, do you feel steady? Or do you feel suspended? After you spend time together, are you grounded? Or analyzing tone, timing, and subtext?

Friendship should not feel like emotional negotiation. It should not feel like you are managing your own expectations in silence. It should not feel like you are trying to be evolved while quietly waiting for something to shift.

A healthy friendship does not require self-suppression. It allows space without strategy. It allows care without claim. It allows presence without possession.

The disruptive truth is this: if the label "friend" stabilizes you, then it may be real. But if the label "friend" feels like something you are trying to accept rather than something you genuinely embody, then the dynamic has not fully transformed.

Friendship in a twin flame connection is not about proximity. It is about freedom.

If you feel truly free and at ease in the friendship, it is healthy. If you act as if you are free but, inside, still feel the need to please or hold on, it is more about attachment than real freedom.

And only you can tell the difference.

Chapter 33

When Emotion Feels Like Truth

In a twin flame dynamic, emotion does not arrive gently. It arrives amplified. What might have been a small reaction in another relationship becomes a tidal wave here. Longing feels deeper. Joy feels brighter. Rejection feels sharper. Silence feels louder.

And because the emotion is intense, the mind assumes it must mean something extraordinary.

We analyze every word. Every pause. Every delay. We search for spiritual, psychological, and cosmic explanations. The mind tries to stabilize what the body is feeling.

But emotion, by nature, is temporary.

It rises.
It peaks.
It falls.

The intensity of the feeling does not always determine the permanence of the connection. Sometimes it simply reveals how deeply you are capable of feeling.

In this dynamic, emotion becomes a mirror. Not because it proves destiny. But because it exposes sensitivity, attachment, desire, and fear. The mistake is not feeling deeply. The mistake is believing every emotion is a prophecy.

When you begin to see emotion as experience rather than instruction, something softens. You can feel fully without constructing a future from every wave.

Emotion becomes part of the curriculum of being human.

Not proof of eternal union. Not evidence of illusion.

Just experience.

And experience, when observed instead of dramatized, becomes **wisdom.**

Chapter 34

Why the Magnetism Feels Ancient

There are connections that grow slowly, and there are connections that arrive fully formed.

With some people, you build familiarity over time. You learn their patterns. You collect shared experiences. You develop closeness through repetition.

But a twin flame dynamic often feels inverted.

The familiarity is immediate.

You look at them, and something in you relaxes or ignites. Conversation feels strangely effortless, or electrically charged. Silence feels loaded, not empty. You may even feel as though you are remembering something rather than discovering it.

This is what many describe as "past life recognition."

Whether that memory is literal or symbolic is less important than what it reveals.

At a soul level, recognition is not about history. It is about resonance.

Your soul carries a frequency. When another person vibrates at a compatible or complementary frequency, your system registers it before your mind understands it. That registration can feel like:

"I know you."
"I have been here before."
"This feels familiar."

Familiar does not always mean safe. It means resonant.

This is why the magnetism feels ancient.

Not because you necessarily shared a castle in another century, though some believe that. It feels ancient because the connection bypasses the surface personality and touches something deeper.

It touches a pattern. It touches an archetype. It touches unfinished growth.

When this happens, the nervous system reacts intensely. The mind tries to interpret it. The ego wants to secure it. But the soul is not concerned with securing.

The soul is concerned with evolution.

This is also why separation feels so destabilizing. When a connection touches you at that depth, it exposes attachments you did not know you carried. It reveals desires you had buried. It confronts fears you had avoided.

The magnetism is not just attraction. It is acceleration.

And acceleration can feel like destiny, but acceleration can also be curriculum.

Some twin flames are meant to stay in romantic union. Some are meant to catalyze each other into higher alignment and then release. The intensity does not determine the duration. It determines the depth of awakening.

When you understand this, the ancient feeling stops being proof of possession. It becomes proof of activation.

And activation, even when it hurts, is sacred.

Chapter 35

The Power Was Never Outside You

At first, the connection feels external. The energy seems to come from the other person. Their presence shifts you. Their absence destabilizes you. You measure your emotional state by their behavior.

It is easy to believe they are the source.

But over time, if you are paying attention, something changes.

You begin to notice that the intensity you once attributed to them is still alive even when they are not physically present. The creativity continues. The spiritual curiosity deepens. The emotional awareness expands.

The power did not leave.

It moved inward.

This is the turning point in the twin flame journey. When you realize the connection didn't give you energy, it reveals itself.

At first, the dynamic feels like attachment. Then it feels like an obsession. Then it feels like destiny. But eventually, if you allow it to mature, it becomes initiation.

An initiation into yourself.

This is why twin flame work is inward work. Not because you are meant to analyze endlessly. Not because you are meant to suffer. But because the intensity forces you to confront what lives inside you.

Unhealed wounds surface.
    Hidden desires surface.
        Suppressed power surfaces.

The person becomes secondary. The awakening becomes primary.

Some will surrender to the connection and stay in the outer dynamic. Others will surrender inward and discover that the real union was never about possession.

It was about integration.

And integration does not remove love.

It removes dependency.

Chapter 36

Loving Without Needing the Outcome

There is a version of love that feels desperate for a conclusion. It wants clarity. It wants labels. It wants guarantees. It wants to know where it is going and how it will end.

And yet, there exists another version of love altogether.

It is quieter.

It does not collapse if the other person steps away. It does not panic when timing shifts. It does not measure its worth by reciprocation.

It simply loves.

This stage is not easy to reach. It usually comes after the intensity has burned through you. After the questions. After the analysis. After the emotional waves. At some point, exhaustion turns into awareness.

You realize that your capacity to love is not dependent on the outcome. I did not arrive here quickly. There were moments of longing, moments of confusion, moments of trying to understand what the connection meant. But eventually, something inside me stabilized.

I could feel the bond without trying to control it.

That is when love changes form.

It stops being about possession. It stops being about securing the future. It stops being about whether they choose you.

It becomes an expression of who you are.

You can care deeply and still go on with your life. You can feel warmth without needing reassurance. You can hold the memory without clinging to the person.

This is not detachment in the cold sense. It is detachment in the sovereign sense.

You are no longer bargaining with destiny.

You are no longer asking, "Will this become a union?"

You are asking, "Can I remain whole regardless?"

And when the answer becomes yes, something profound happens.

The energy shifts from craving to calm. From urgency to steadiness. From fantasy to presence.

You stop needing the story to end in a specific way. You stop trying to script eternity. Love remains, but it is no longer heavy.

It feels spacious.

In this space, you can choose again. You can build a life. You can meet new people. You can laugh. You can travel. You can evolve. And none of it betrays the depth you once felt.

Because loving without needing the outcome is not about losing hope.
It is about gaining freedom.

And freedom is the highest expression of love.

Chapter 37

When the Connection Becomes Your Fuel

There are moments when you realize the connection is no longer just about the person. It has become energy. It fuels your thoughts. It fuels your creativity. It fuels your emotional depth. It even fuels your sense of being alive.

Without it, you fear you might become flat.

This is rarely spoken out loud, but it is common.

Some people do not want to let go of the connection because it is the first time they have felt fully awake.

Before it, life may have been steady but muted. Predictable but uninspired. Functional but emotionally contained.

Then the magnetism arrives.

Suddenly, colors feel sharper. Music feels deeper. Writing flows. Spiritual curiosity expands. You feel more than you have in years.

It is not only about the other person.

It is about the intensity you discovered inside yourself.

This is where decoding becomes essential.

Is the person fueling you?

Or did the connection unlock something that was already dormant within you?

If the energy lives only in them, you will chase it, but if the energy is activated within you, then you carry it.

Some twin flame dynamics are not here to stay physically. They are here to awaken capacity.

And once awakened, that capacity does not disappear unless you hand it back.

For some, surrender is the next natural phase. They surrender to the intensity, to the unfolding, and to not knowing the outcome.

For others, the connection becomes identity.

And identity is harder to let go of than love.

This book does not tell you to detach. It invites you to observe.

Is the connection expanding you? Or are you shrinking around it?

Is it fueling your evolution? Or replacing your center?

The answer is not universal.

But it is knowable. You must be willing to look without romanticizing or demonizing.

Sometimes the twin flame is not meant to be removed.

It is meant to be integrated.

And integration feels very different from obsession.

Chapter 38

The Inner World Where It All Lives

At some point in the twin flame journey, a quiet realization begins to form. The intensity, the longing, the expansion, the ache — none of it exists "out there" in the way you first believed. It exists in your inner world.

This does not make the connection imaginary. It makes it personal.

Two people can share the same experience and walk away carrying completely different internal realities. One may feel awakened. The other may feel overwhelmed. One may feel destiny. The other may feel curiosity. The event was shared. The meaning was not.

The twin flame dynamic often feels cosmic because it collapses perception and emotion into something larger than life. But what is actually happening is deeply human. Your nervous system is activated. Your identity is reorganizing. Your inner architecture is expanding.

The other person is the catalyst.

The transformation is yours.

When you locate the experience inside yourself, something stabilizes. You stop needing outside confirmation to validate what you feel. You stop measuring the connection by their response. You understand that the intensity was real because it moved through you.

This realization is not dismissive. It is empowering.

It means the awakening did not belong to them. It belonged to you.

And if the activation lived inside you, then the integration lives inside you, too.

The dynamic may continue, evolve, or dissolve. But the expansion remains yours.

That is where sovereignty begins.

Chapter 39

The Soul Contract You Don't Remember Signing

There are connections that feel accidental, and others that feel orchestrated.

A twin flame dynamic rarely feels random. It arrives with timing that is almost suspicious. It activates you in ways that feel disproportionate to the amount of time you have known each other. It feels ancient, immediate, and irreversible.

From a spiritual perspective, some souls agree to meet before they incarnate. Not to complete each other. Not to rescue each other. But to awaken each other.

A soul contract is not romantic. It is evolutionary.

You do not meet to live happily ever after. You meet to remember who you are.

And remembering is rarely gentle.

Sometimes the contract is simple: "I will trigger you into expansion."

Sometimes it is more complex: "I will mirror your unfinished lessons until you integrate them."

This is why twin flame connections often arrive when you are on the edge of a personal shift. You may be stable. You may be successful. You may even be content. And then suddenly, everything feels rearranged.

But the person did not rearrange you.

The agreement did.

And here is the part most people misunderstand: A soul contract does not guarantee physical union.

It guarantees activation.

Some souls agree to walk together for a lifetime. Some agree to collide for a season. Some agree to awaken each other and then separate.

The duration does not determine the depth.

When you look at your connection through this lens, the desperation softens. The obsession shifts. Instead of asking, "Will we end up together?" you begin asking, "What did we agree to awaken in each other?"

That question changes everything.

Because if the contract was to awaken your sovereignty, then clinging violates it.

If the contract was to awaken your heart, then closing it violates it.

If the contract was to activate your mission, then stagnating after the activation misses the point.

You may not remember signing anything before this life. But your soul remembers the growth.

And sometimes that is enough.

However, there are twin flames who build lives together. There are twin flames who marry, raise families, and walk side by side in physical union. Romance is not excluded from the spiritual path. Love, in its embodied form, can be sacred.

But many connections that feel like twin flames are evolutionary first, romantic second.

The purpose is not always to stay.

The purpose is often to awaken.

When you approach the dynamic this way, you stop measuring the connection by outcome. You begin measuring it by transformation.

Did you grow?
Did you expand?
Did you confront parts of yourself you had avoided?
Did your consciousness widen?

If the answer is yes, the contract has already fulfilled its sacred function regardless of whether the relationship became permanent.

This perspective does not limit belief. It liberates it.

Because now romance is possible, but it is not required for meaning.

Union is beautiful, but evolution is the constant.

And evolution does not depend on another person staying.

Chapter 40

Parallel Growth Even When Apart

There is a quiet phase in the twin flame dynamic that doesn't look dramatic from the outside. No declarations. No intense arguments. No passionate reunions. Just distance. Sometimes physical. Sometimes emotional. Sometimes both.

And yet, something is still moving.

This is the part many people misunderstand. They assume that if communication slows down or stops, the growth stops too. They assume that if they are not actively interacting, the connection has paused.

But growth does not require proximity.

I did not understand this at first. When the distance appeared, I thought something had broken. I thought the connection was weakening, fading, dissolving into memory. But what I slowly realized was that something inside me was still evolving even when she was not physically present.

I was thinking differently. Responding differently. Making choices I would not have made before.

The external interaction may have quieted, but the internal transformation did not.

That is parallel growth.

It is when two people, connected by something deeper than ordinary attraction, continue evolving on separate paths. Not in competition. Not in synchronization. Just in motion.

You may not know what the other person is doing. They may not tell you. They may even appear detached. But something in you continues expanding, and that expansion is not dependent on their daily presence.

This is where the connection becomes mature.

It is no longer about constant reassurance. It is no longer about chasing contact or analyzing every message. It becomes quieter. More stable. Less reactive.

You begin building your life. They begin building theirs.

And strangely, the bond does not feel weaker. It feels steadier.

Parallel growth does not guarantee reunion. It does not promise romance. It does not ensure timing will align. What it offers instead is something subtler: dignity.

You are no longer shrinking while waiting. You are not suspending your evolution until they catch up. You are not pausing your expansion for the sake of potential.

You are living.

And if the connection is truly sacred, it does not require you to stop becoming yourself.

It becomes a background frequency rather than a constant interruption.

There is a maturity in this stage that feels different from intensity. It is less intoxicating but more grounded. You can love without collapsing. You can remember without obsessing. You can care without chasing.

Growth continues. On both sides.

Whether you see it or not.

And if one day your paths cross again, you will not meet as the same versions who once struggled. You will meet people who have lived, learned, and expanded.

And if they do not cross again, the growth was never wasted.

Because what changed was you.

Chapter 41

How Souls Recognize Each Other

There is a moment in some connections that cannot be explained logically. It happens before labels. Before definitions. Before anyone says "twin flame." It happens in the body first.

You meet someone, and something in you responds — not loudly, not always dramatically, but unmistakably.

It can feel like a subtle click, a gentle expansion in the chest, a natural pull, or a quiet current.

The mind tries to categorize it as an attraction. Chemistry. Curiosity. But the experience often feels deeper than that. It feels as though something in you has been waiting.

Spiritual traditions describe this as soul recognition.

Not recognition of personality, but recognition of frequency.

Every human carries a field. A pattern of memory, emotion, experience, belief, and energetic imprint. Most interactions remain at the surface level of personality. But occasionally, someone's field touches yours at a depth that bypasses performance.

You feel seen before you explain yourself. You feel exposed without being attacked. You feel understood without presenting evidence.

This is why twin flame connections can feel ancient.

It is not always about past-life memory. It is about resonance.

When two fields carry complementary patterns — similar wounds, mirrored strengths, compatible evolution points they create a charge. That charge can feel like destiny. It can feel like inevitability. It can feel like you are stepping into something prewritten.

But recognition does not automatically equal compatibility.

Souls may recognize each other long before the human personalities are capable of sustaining each other.

This is where confusion begins.

You may feel at home in someone's presence, yet destabilized by their behavior. You may feel deeply connected and yet chronically uncertain. You may feel spiritually aligned and emotionally mismatched.

Recognition is the opening.

Evolution is the process.

Some souls meet to remember who they were before conditioning. Others meet to confront patterns they have been avoiding. A few meet to build something together in the physical world.

And some meet simply to awaken each other into a new stage of consciousness.

The recognition itself is not the final destination.

It is the doorway.

The mistake many make is assuming that because something feels ancient, it must last forever.

Sometimes the ancient feeling exists to accelerate growth, not to secure permanence.

When you understand this, the magnetism stops feeling like a trap.

It becomes a teacher.

Chapter 42

The Aha — Watching Yourself From Above

There is a moment in every intense connection when the "story," the narrative you tell yourself about the relationship, cracks open. This doesn't happen because the other person changes or because the ending becomes obvious. It happens when your perspective on the connection shifts.

You begin to sense that you are both the character and the observer. You are the one longing, reacting, analyzing, and decoding, and you are also the awareness watching it all unfold.

From inside the dynamic, it feels like a story being written for you, an inevitable unfolding.

From slightly above it, it feels like a curriculum.

And that realization does not diminish the depth of what you felt. It reframes it.

Imagine, just for a moment, that there is a layer of you beyond personality — beyond attachment style, beyond ego, beyond fear. Call it higher self, 5D awareness, soul perspective, the language does not matter. What matters is the shift.

From that vantage point, nothing is dramatic.

It sees two incarnated beings navigating polarity. It sees activation triggering evolution. It sees longing exposing attachment. It sees distance teaching as self-contained. It sees intensity refining discipline.
It does not see tragedy.
It sees learning.

And sometimes, when you access that altitude, something unexpected happens.

You stop asking, "Will this work out?"

You start asking, "What did this awaken in me?"

You stop needing the other person to validate the experience.

You recognize that the awakening occurred inside your own consciousness.

And here is the expansive truth:

If twin flames exist at a higher dimensional level, they are not trapped in push–pull. They are not anxious. They are not avoiding. They are not strategizing texts.

They are whole.

It is only here, inside embodiment, that polarity becomes friction. Where memory becomes longing. Where identity becomes attachment.

From above, it may look almost beautiful.

Two humans stumbling through intensity, calling it destiny, resisting it, surrendering to it, labeling it, spiritualizing it all, while slowly learning sovereignty.

And perhaps that is the Aha.

Maybe the real Aha is this: You are here to learn sovereignty, not to guarantee togetherness.

Not that the bond is an illusion, but the entire experience was an initiation.

An initiation into self-awareness. An initiation into discipline. An initiation into loving without collapse. An initiation into seeing clearly without losing depth.

When you gain this higher perspective on the dynamic, you don't detach from it.

You integrate it.

You can laugh gently at your own urgency. You can forgive your own obsession. You can respect the other person's limitations. You can continue your expansion without resentment.

That's when you begin to understand: the lesson was never about securing the bond.

It was about strengthening the self.

And from that awareness, the dynamic no longer controls you.

It becomes part of your evolution.

Chapter 43

The Mission You Don't Have to Prove

When I first heard that some twin flames are here on a mission to change the Earth's energy, I felt a quiet recognition.

Part of me understood the language. The connection had felt larger than romance. It had disrupted my inner world. It had ignited creativity, forced growth, and awakened parts of me that had been dormant for years. Something shifted permanently. That kind of shift does not feel small.

Some twin flames are conscious of a shared purpose. They build something together. They teach, create, serve, or anchor something visible in the world.

But many never speak about a mission. They just collide. They just awaken. They just transform.

And sometimes the mission is not between the two of you.

Sometimes the mission is what the connection awakens inside you.

When I encountered this connection, I did not have a twin flame vocabulary. I did not even know what that meant. I only knew something in me had shifted so dramatically that I could not ignore it.
It led me to search.

That search led me into regression.

Regression led me into a larger narrative. It included past lives, Earth participation, and a sense of having chosen this incarnation for specific growth.

Not everyone will go that route. Not everyone needs to.

Some people will experience this dynamic without ever using the word twin flame. Some will never explore regression. Some will never conceptualize it as a mission.

And that does not invalidate their experience.

The depth you access depends on your own spiritual architecture.

For some, the connection awakens curiosity. For others, it awakens healing. For others, it awakens creativity. For a few, it awakens memory.

The point is not to assign a universal spiritual story.

The point is to acknowledge that for some souls, this dynamic opens doors they did not know existed.

And for others, it simply teaches them self-worth.

Both are valid.

Chapter 44

Now That You See It

Maybe you're reading this with a cup of coffee in your hand. Maybe it's afternoon tea. Maybe it's late at night, and the house is quiet. Maybe you're still in the middle of your own dynamic, or maybe you're in the stillness after it.

Wherever you are, notice something.

The intensity you once couldn't control… is now something you can observe.

The obsession that once felt like gravity… is now something you can name.

The longing that once dictated your mood… is now something you can hold without collapsing.

That shift did not happen because the other person changed.

It happened because you saw it.

You decoded it.

And now, sitting here in your ordinary moment — reading words, sipping something warm, breathing without urgency, you can appreciate the experience differently.

Not as a trap. Not as a destiny to secure. Not as a story to defend.

But as a chapter you lived.

You can look at the stillness and recognize its peace. You can look at the obsession and recognize its lesson. You can look at the push–pull and recognize your own growth inside it.

The twin flame dynamic may have felt cosmic.

But this moment is human.

And it is powerful because now you are not inside the storm.

You are aware of it.

And awareness is freedom.

Whether you continue the connection or not, whether it evolves or dissolves, you are no longer operating blindly. You are no longer reacting without reflection. You are no longer mistaking activation for destiny.

You are present.

And from presence, everything feels different.

Even coffee tastes different when you are not waiting for a text.

Even silence feels lighter when you are not measuring it.

Even love feels cleaner when it is not tangled with fear.

That may be the quietest Aha of all.

Not that the connection was meant to last forever in the 3D world.

But that it was meant to awaken you.

And now you are awake.

Chapter 45

Conscious Union vs Eternal Bond

There is a subtle confusion that lives inside the twin flame narrative. The belief is that if something feels eternal, it must also manifest permanently in the physical world.

But eternity and permanence are not the same thing.

When we speak of an eternal bond, we mean recognition. A familiarity that does not need introduction. A depth that feels older than this lifetime. It is the kind of connection that bypasses logic and goes straight to knowing.

You meet them, and something inside you says, "I remember."

That remembering can be powerful enough to shake your entire sense of reality. It can awaken parts of you that were dormant. It can reorient your life, your beliefs, your priorities. The bond feels undeniable because it touches something timeless.

But an eternal bond does not automatically equal conscious union. Conscious union is different.

Conscious union requires two individuals who are both aware of themselves. Two people who have faced their shadows. Two people who have chosen growth over avoidance. It requires emotional maturity, communication, stability, and willingness.

An eternal bond is recognition. Conscious union is participation.

One can exist without the other.

This is where many people get trapped. They assume that because the bond feels ancient, the union must be destined. They hold onto intensity as proof. They interpret synchronicities as confirmation. They believe that if something feels cosmic, it must conclude in partnership.

But consciousness is choice.

Even two souls who share a deep bond can choose different paths in a lifetime. They can awaken each other without walking side by side forever. They can trigger evolution without signing a contract of permanence.

This does not make the bond less sacred.

It makes it free.

There is something profoundly mature about understanding this distinction. You can honor the eternal without demanding it materialize exactly as you imagine. You can acknowledge the depth without forcing it into structure.

And sometimes, conscious union does happen. Sometimes, both individuals grow into the same level of awareness at the same time. Sometimes timing aligns. Sometimes the bond and the maturity meet. But when they do, it is not because destiny forced it. It is because both chose it.

That is the difference.

Eternal bonds are about memory. Conscious union is about readiness.

One is timeless.

The other is intentional.

And when you understand this, you stop clinging. You stop bargaining with the universe. You stop trying to prove the connection.

With this understanding, your perspective shifts, and you begin asking a different question.

Not "Is this eternal?"

But "Are we both conscious enough to build something stable?"

The answer may not always be yes.

And that does not diminish what was felt.

Some bonds arrive simply to awaken you.

Some are here to partner.

Some are here to teach you what you are capable of loving.

And in the end, sometimes the most sacred part of the journey is realizing you can honor the eternity without sacrificing your present life to it.

Chapter 46

The Role of Consciousness in Twin Flame Experiences

At some point in this journey, the focus shifts from the other person to awareness itself.

You begin to observe your own reactions. You notice how thoughts amplify emotion. You recognize how attachment narratives form. You see how identity gets entangled with the story of "us."

This is where decoding becomes deeper than the relationship.

It becomes conscious work.

You realize that the twin flame dynamic is not happening to you; it is happening within you.

The magnetism, the longing, the recognition, the fear, all of it is processed through your awareness. Two people can experience the same connection in completely different ways because consciousness interprets reality uniquely.

The connection becomes a mirror not only of emotion, but of perception.

What you believe about love will color what you experience. What you fear about abandonment will influence how you respond. What you expect from destiny will shape what you notice.

The twin flame becomes less of a person and more of a catalyst for self-awareness.

This is why some people grow, and others loop.

Growth requires observation.

When you observe your thoughts instead of immediately believing them, the intensity softens. Similarly, when you witness your emotions rather than react to them, clarity arises.

Through these practices, consciousness creates space.

And in that space, something quietly revolutionary emerges: You are participating in it.

This does not make it less sacred. It makes it more deliberate.

You are not here to be overwhelmed. You are here to become aware. And awareness is the real union.

This union is not necessarily with another person,

But with yourself.

Chapter 47

You Are Not the Story — You Are the Awareness Experiencing It

At some point, after all the decoding, something becomes very clear.

The twin flame experience feels enormous while you are inside it. It feels like the center of your world. It shapes your thoughts, your emotions, your decisions. It can feel like destiny itself.

But when you step back, when awareness expands, you begin to see something else.

You are not the story.

You are the awareness experiencing the story.

This distinction changes everything.

The connection may feel eternal. The bond may feel cosmic. The intensity may feel overwhelming. But none of it exists outside of your consciousness. It is all being perceived, interpreted, and lived through you.

Consciousness is the constant.

The relationship is the event.

And when you realize this, the hierarchy shifts.

You are not at the mercy of the bond. You are not trapped inside a dynamic. You are not a victim of timing or fate. You are the awareness within which all of this is unfolding.

The push and pull.
   The longing.
      The awakening.
         The silence.
            The union.
               The separation.

All of it moves through consciousness.

Yet, consciousness alone persists throughout it all.

This is not detachment in a cold sense. It is an expansion. You begin to feel less identified with the emotional waves and more anchored in the space that observes them.

Through this expanded awareness, you experience love without being consumed by it. You feel depth without losing stability and remember eternity without abandoning the present.

The twin flame becomes part of your human experience, not the definition of your existence.

From this realization, true sovereignty begins to emerge.

When you recognize yourself as awareness, you realize: Nothing controls you.

Everything is here to reveal you.

The connection is not meant to reduce you to longing. It is meant to expand your perception, to show your emotional depth, spiritual sensitivity, and capacity for growth.

But you were always larger than the story.

You were always the consciousness witnessing it.

And when you settle into that recognition, the entire journey softens.

Not because it disappears.

But because you are no longer inside it as a character trying to survive the plot.

You are the awareness that can experience it fully and still remain whole.

Chapter 48

There Is No Final Answer

If you came here looking for certainty, I understand. I did too. I wanted to know if the connection was real, if it would last, if it meant something eternal. I wanted an answer that would quiet the mind and settle the heart.

But the twin flame journey does not offer final answers. It offers awareness.

Some connections become lifelong partnerships. Some become friendships. Some dissolve. Some return years later in a completely different form. Some remain as quiet imprints that permanently reshaped you.

There is no single ending that proves the bond was authentic because the twin flame dynamic is not a destination you arrive at. It is an experience you move through.

A journey does not exist to give you a trophy at the end. It exists to change you while you walk it.

For some, that change includes romance. For others, it includes spiritual growth. For many, it includes both at different times.

The mistake is believing that union is the only successful outcome.

The deeper truth is that expansion is.

If the connection made you more self-aware, more disciplined, more sovereign, more conscious of your patterns, more honest about your desires, then it fulfilled its purpose.

Whether it stays or leaves becomes secondary.

You do not need to be an expert to know what you lived. You do not need to prove the existence of twin flames to anyone. You only need to know whether you are awake inside your own experience.

And that is something no one else can define for you.

The journey continues, not because you are unfinished, but because growth never stops.

There is no final answer.

Only moments.

And how consciously you choose to live them.

For some, the twin flame journey includes partnership. For others, it includes transformation. And for a few, it may include something that feels like a shared mission — a purpose that extends beyond romance. I cannot define that for you. I am simply someone living it, observing it, decoding it in real time.

We are all in this journey. I am writing from awareness. And I stand by what I lived.

Epilogue

Open Sky

If you are looking for a final answer in the 3D world, I don't have a specific one.

And perhaps, this search for certainty is the heart of the journey.

The 3D mind loves destinations. It wants to know whether this is forever, whether it will end, whether this bond is eternal or temporary. It wants certainty so it can rest.

But the twin flame journey, or whatever name you give to a connection that rearranges you, does not move in straight lines. It unfolds in layers. It evolves. It pauses. It intensifies. It softens.

Sometimes it looks like romance. Sometimes it looks like friendship. Sometimes it looks like distance. Sometimes it looks like a purpose.

Nothing is promised.

And it's this very uncertainty that makes it sacred.

Maybe some bonds are eternal. Not in the way the ego imagines, not always in proximity, not always in partnership, but in imprint. In memory. In the way they change the architecture of who we are.

Maybe this is an eternal bond.

Or maybe it is an eternal lesson.

Or maybe it is both.

Like you. I am living this and observing it, just as you are. I have not completed the journey. I am inside it learning, integrating, decoding.

And perhaps that is enough.

There is no final destination to arrive at. There is only awareness expanding through experience.

Your 3D mind may still want closure.

But your deeper self is learning something more powerful:

To stay present without guarantee.

To love without collapse.

To grow without waiting.

To live fully even when the story is still unfolding.

The journey does not end here.

It simply continues with you more conscious than before.

And maybe that is the real **union**.

The Language of the Journey

A Twin Flame Decoder

173

Twin Flame

A connection that feels larger than romance. It activates parts of you that were dormant. It often feels destined. It is, at its core, a mirror.

Activation

The moment your emotional world shifts. You cannot go back to who you were before this person. Something has been awakened — not in them, but in you.

Chaser

The one who becomes conscious first. The one who feels the intensity and seeks clarity. This is not weakness. It is awareness arriving early.

Runner

The one who feels the same intensity but does not yet have the capacity to hold it. Distance is often a nervous system response, not lack of feeling.

(Still stabilizing…)

Push–Pull

The cycle of closeness and distance. It feels mystical. Sometimes it is. Sometimes it is two nervous systems dysregulated and calling it fate.

(Gently disruptive begins…)

Trauma Bond

When attachment is fueled by wounds rather than growth. If your identity begins shrinking, waiting, or collapsing — pause. Not everything intense is sacred.

Sacred Bond

A connection that expands you even when it challenges you. You may ache, but you do not disappear.

Stillness

The phase when obsession softens and self returns. This is not the end of love. It is the return of sovereignty.

Union

Not always physical. Not always romantic. Sometimes union is the integration of the parts of you that were activated by the mirror.